TREATING
PRESCHOOL CHILDREN

THE JOSSEY-BASS LIBRARY OF CURRENT CLINICAL TECHNIQUE

IRVIN D. YALOM, GENERAL EDITOR

NOW AVAILABLE

Treating Alcoholism
Stephanie Brown, Editor

Treating Schizophrenia
Sophia Vinogradov, Editor

Treating Women Molested in Childhood
Catherine Classen, Editor

Treating Depression
Ira D. Glick, Editor

Treating Eating Disorders
Joellen Werne, Editor

Treating Dissociative Identity Disorder
James L. Spira, Editor

Treating Couples
Hilda Kessler, Editor

Treating Adolescents
Hans Steiner, Editor

Treating the Elderly
Javaid I. Sheikh, Editor

Treating Sexual Disorders
Randolph S. Charlton, Editor

Treating Difficult Personality Disorders
Michael Rosenbluth, Editor

Treating Anxiety Disorders
Walton T. Roth, Editor

Treating the Psychological Consequences of HIV
Michael F. O'Connor, Editor

Treating Preschool Children
Hans Steiner, Editor

Treating School-Age Children
Hans Steiner, Editor

TREATING
PRESCHOOL CHILDREN

A VOLUME IN THE JOSSEY-BASS
LIBRARY OF CURRENT CLINICAL TECHNIQUE

Hans Steiner, EDITOR

Irvin D. Yalom, GENERAL EDITOR

Jossey-Bass Publishers • San Francisco

Substantial discounts on bulk quantities of Jossey-Bass books are available to corporations, professional associations, and other organizations. For details and discount information, contact the special sales department at Jossey-Bass Inc., Publishers (415) 433–1740; Fax (800) 605–2665.

For sales outside the United States, please contact your local Simon & Schuster International Office.

Jossey-Bass Web address: http://www.josseybass.com

 Manufactured in the United States of America on Lyons Falls Turin Book. This paper is acid-free and 100 percent totally chlorine-free.

Library of Congress Cataloging-in-Publication Data

Treating preschool children/Hans Steiner, editor; Irvin D. Yalom, general editor.
    p.   cm.—(A volume in the Jossey-Bass library of current clinical technique)
Includes bibliographical references and index.
ISBN 0-7879-0877-0 (alk. paper)
1. Preschool children—Mental health. 2. Child psychiatry. I. Steiner, Hans, date. II. Yalom, Irvin D., date. III. Series: Jossey-Bass library of current clinical technique.
RJ499.T82 1997
618.92'89—dc21
                                             97-20811
                                               CIP

FIRST EDITION
PB Printing 10 9 8 7 6 5 4 3 2 1

CONTENTS

FOREWORD

At a recent meeting of clinical practitioners, a senior practitioner declared that more change had occurred in his practice of psychotherapy in the past year than in the twenty preceding years. Nodding assent, the others all agreed.

And was that a good thing for their practice? A resounding "No!" Again, unanimous concurrence—too much interference from managed care; too much bureaucracy; too much paperwork; too many limits set on fees, length, and format of therapy; too much competition from new psychotherapy professions.

Were these changes a good or a bad thing for the general public? Less unanimity on this question. Some pointed to recent positive developments. Psychotherapy was becoming more mainstream, more available, and more acceptable to larger segments of the American public. It was being subjected to closer scrutiny and accountability—uncomfortable for the practitioner but, if done properly, of potential benefit to the quality and efficiency of behavioral health care delivery.

But without dissent this discussion group agreed—and every aggregate of therapists would concur—that astounding changes are looming for our profession: changes in the reasons that clients request therapy; changes in the perception and practice of mental health care; changes in therapeutic theory and technique; and changes in the training, certification, and supervision of professional therapists.

From the perspective of the clientele, several important currents are apparent. A major development is the de-stigmatization of psychotherapy. No longer is psychotherapy invariably a hush-hush affair, laced with shame and conducted in offices with separate entrance and exit doors to prevent the uncomfortable possibility of clients meeting one another.

Today such shame and secrecy have been exploded. Television talk shows—Oprah, Geraldo, Donahue—have normalized psychopathology and psychotherapy by presenting a continuous public parade of dysfunctional human situations: hardly a day passes without television fare of confessions and audience interactions with deadbeat fathers, sex addicts, adult children of alcoholics, battering husbands and abused wives, drug dealers and substance abusers, food bingers and purgers, thieving children, abusing parents, victimized children suing parents.

The implications of such de-stigmatization have not been lost on professionals who no longer concentrate their efforts on the increasingly elusive analytically suitable neurotic patient. Clinics everywhere are dealing with a far broader spectrum of problem areas and must be prepared to offer help to substance abusers and their families, to patients with a wide variety of eating disorders, adult survivors of incest, victims and perpetrators of domestic abuse. No longer do trauma victims or substance abusers furtively seek counseling. Public awareness of the noxious long-term effects of trauma has been so sensitized that there is an increasing call for public counseling facilities and a growing demand, as well, for adequate counseling provisions in health care plans.

The mental health profession is changing as well. No longer is there such automatic adoration of lengthy "depth" psychotherapy where "deep" or "profound" is equated with a focus on the earliest years of the patient's life. The contemporary field is more pluralistic: many diverse approaches have proven therapeutically effective and the therapist of today is more apt to tailor the therapy to fit the particular clinical needs of each patient.

In past years there was an unproductive emphasis on territoriality and on the maintaining of hierarchy and status—with the more prestigious professions like psychiatry and doctoral-level psychology expending considerable energy toward excluding master's level therapists. But those battles belong more to the psychotherapists of yesterday; today there is a significant shift toward a more collaborative interdisciplinary climate.

Managed care and cost containment are driving some of these changes. The role of the psychiatrist has been particularly affected as cost efficiency has decreed that psychiatrists will less frequently deliver psychotherapy personally but, instead, limit their activities to supervision and to psychopharmacological treatment.

In its efforts to contain costs, managed care has asked therapists to deliver a briefer, focused therapy. But gradually managed care is realizing that the bulk of mental health treatment cost is consumed by inpatient care and that outpatient treatment, even long-term therapy, is not only salubrious for the patient but far less costly. Another looming change is that the field is turning more frequently toward the group therapies. How much longer can we ignore the many comparative research studies demonstrating that the group therapy format is equally or more effective than higher cost individual therapies?

Some of these cost-driven edicts may prove to be good for the patients; but many of the changes that issue from medical model mimicry—for example, efforts at extreme brevity and overly precise treatment plans and goals that are inappropriate to the therapy endeavor and provide only the illusion of efficiency—can hamper the therapeutic work. Consequently, it is of paramount importance that therapists gain control of their field and that managed care administrators not be permitted to dictate how psychotherapy or, for that matter, any other form of health care be conducted. That is one of the goals of this series of texts: to provide mental health professionals with such a deep grounding in theory and such a clear vision of effective therapeutic technique that they will be empowered to fight confidently for the highest standards of patient care.

The Jossey-Bass Library of Current Clinical Technique is directed and dedicated to the frontline therapist—to master's and doctoral-level clinicians who personally provide the great bulk of mental health care. The purpose of this entire series is to offer state-of-the-art instruction in treatment techniques for the most commonly encountered clinical conditions. Each volume offers a focused theoretical background as a foundation for practice and then dedicates itself to the practical task of what to do for the patient—how to assess, diagnose, and treat.

I have selected volume editors who are either nationally recognized experts or are rising young stars. In either case, they possess a comprehensive view of their specialty field and have selected leading therapists of a variety of persuasions to describe their therapeutic approaches.

Although all the contributors have incorporated the most recent and relevant clinical research in their chapters, the emphasis in these volumes is the practical technique of therapy. We shall offer specific therapeutic guidelines, and augment concrete suggestions with the liberal use of clinical vignettes and detailed case histories. Our intention is not to impress or to awe the reader, and not to add footnotes to arcane academic debates. Instead, each chapter is designed to communicate guidelines of immediate pragmatic value to the practicing clinician. In fact, the general editor, the volume editors, and the chapter contributors have all accepted our assignments for that very reason: a rare opportunity to make a significant, immediate, and concrete contribution to the lives of our patients.

Irvin D. Yalom, M.D.
Professor Emeritus of Psychiatry
Stanford University School of Medicine

INTRODUCTION

Hans Steiner

Intimate attachments to other human beings are the hub around which a person's life revolves, not only when he is an infant or a toddler or a schoolchild, but throughout his adolescence and his years of maturity as well, and on into old age. From these intimate attachments, a person draws his strengths and enjoyments in life and, through what he contributes, he gives strength and enjoyment to others. These are matters about which current science and traditional wisdom are at one.

JOHN BOWLBY, *ATTACHMENT AND LOSS*, 1980

The chapters in this book address the preschool-age period, from birth through age five. The comprehensive discussion examines how disorders begin, progress, and later more clearly define themselves in the years beyond infancy and toddlerhood as well.

This is the third volume I have edited on the treatment of children ranging in ages from zero to eighteen and the final volume in The Jossey-Bass Library of Current Clinical Technique. Once again, we have identified disorders that are most likely to appear in the infant and toddler range, although they can also appear later in development. Chapter One provides an overview; it outlines principles of development and treatment for the clinician as they apply to this age group. The following chapters spell out in detail how to proceed in each case.

These early years of human development are truly wondrous: from a small bundle of life springs forth the beginnings of a person. If the emotional climate of adolescence can be compared to the explosion of a dancing star, that of the middle childhood years to a journey of discovery of many secrets in a closed, quiet, orderly world in which magic can change everything, then infancy, the early years, resembles the rapid unfolding of a beautiful life from under the protective umbrella of the family. The unfolding and display of abilities are inextricably tied to other people, first and foremost mothers and fathers. It is only through the act of attachment to those who care that this miraculous unfolding can begin. When it is severely disturbed, many functions do not reach their true potential, as has been shown with several cases of extreme deprivation in childhood. From very early on, humans depend on their social environment to fulfill their genetic potential. Genes and environment work hand in hand, and the debate of nature versus nurture has been silenced by the repeated findings that for most human functions, a protective psychosocial envelope is needed to give birth to what is locked up in our genes.

During these infant and toddler years, our selves do not exist in a consistent form—the theorizing of some early psychoanalytic writers notwithstanding. Much needs to be learned and integrated before we become persons. We have traits that are with us from birth and are quite apparent to sensitive parents within the first few hours after birth, but those are just the earliest blocks of who we are to become—not less, not more. As Daniel Stern's outstanding series of investigations has shown, much of our self is contained in interactions with our caregivers. Interactions with caregivers resemble a carefully choreographed dance, in which the caregiver mirrors the child's actions and movements and through this act gives the child his first sense of self: "So this is what I look like when I do this." Gradually parents complement what their infants communicate, and thus one of the first boundaries is established: "When you are sad and scared, I shall comfort, not be sad and scared."

It is always interesting to observe how much their own actions and achievements are a surprise to the infants themselves, sometimes as much as to those around the baby. At this early age, we are what we do, but our minds and bodies are independent entities that we have yet to learn to master, one function after another, and integrate. We become our selves as we learn to recognize and control our own abilities and skills.

Also impressive is the immediacy with which events affect infants and how openly and rapidly they respond to them. Show an infant a bottle with milk, and if she is hungry, her arms will start waving, and she will make cooing sounds. Infants have little capacity for delayed gratification. Their demands are issued when needed, and if they are not responded to, there will be vociferous reminders that something is awry. Infants react without pretense, defensive only in the most rudimentary fashion. Their motives and wishes are quite transparent, as they are for the most part oblivious to social context. They have no need to disguise what motivates their needs, as there are no multiple irreconcilable demands. There is no need for concealment and deceit. Isn't one the center of the universe?

Only in toddlerhood do we witness the emergence of new phenomena, which will ultimately lead children to develop private lives and personhood: the acquisition of language and symbols, which help disguise and conceal. During toddlerhood, children's innermost thoughts are still transparent, as they voice them in private speech, an important step toward complete internalization of thinking under duress. But soon toddlers will be able to keep things to themselves, and not even a look will give away what they know. They are ready to be more fully socialized. They now have the ability to deny a request or demand, which is an important milestone in development and the beginning of their own determination and free will.

Other important changes take place in toddlerhood. Children experience a rapid increase in their mobility, which brings about independence in an unprecedented fashion and leads to separations from the family. The mastery of advanced means of transportation such as tricycles and even bicycles opens the world in new and scary ways. The Brothers Grimm made a veritable inventory of primitive childhood fears on separation from family, created by children's careless leaving of the familial fold. (Hansel and Gretel is perhaps the best known, but there are countless others in their collection.)

Finally, children learn to say no in a most emphatic way, as parents of toddlers are only too acutely aware. Gone is the playful no of the baby; the toddler has a newfound resoluteness to saying no: "I am drawing a line here." Acquiring control over their own bodily functions, such as elimination, gives toddlers the option to decline to follow a parental request in a most dramatic fashion. The battlegrounds of a parent and toddler will over toilet training have been repeatedly described, but there are numerous others unfolding daily, as many exhausted parents will attest. On the average, a toddler asserts selfness every three minutes a day during the waking hours—an impressive feat. Such assertions of free will are balanced by deeply felt and heartily expressed sentiments of love and attachment, and those go a long way to make parents hold up under the onslaught of these earliest forms of independence.

Such powerful boundaries are possible only because toddlers simultaneously create their own "portable parents": transitional objects such as blankets, fuzzy animals, and other items come to represent those whom they defy with their no's and angry outbursts. Maurice Sendak has captured that moment in children's lives exquisitely in pictures and words: *Where the Wild Things Are* can rapidly make anyone understand what defiance at age three to five feels like.

There are substantial technical challenges in preparing to intervene in this age group. What is required of us as clinicians, as we diagnose and treat children in this age range, is the ability to observe subtle cycles of interaction between child and caregivers, child and ourselves. We need to be receptive and still, and we need to respect the patient's vulnerability. At all times, we need to involve the parents, and we need to make them feel in charge of the situation. Selma Fraiberg, one of the founders of infant psychiatry, was a master of this. Her work can serve as an excellent introduction to this field.

We always recommend to therapists that you immerse yourself in your own early past: review of home movies and baby books will quickly bring you in touch with the pace and the emotional flavor with which life flows at this age. It is a life inhabited by giants and gigantic fears, because the children are so little and so relatively powerless. Pleasures are simple and repeat themselves, many, many times before they grow tiring. And when small children are sad, such an emotion wipes out all else in their lives.

Books are useful too to get the clinician in touch with this age group. My own favorites are Hoban's *Frances* stories, which accurately describe the themes of early childhood: greed, fear of the night, competition with babies, comfort in mother's stories. The *Just So* stories by Rudyard Kipling are a more exotic introduction to childhood experiences but just as useful, and the Brothers Grimm have provided the most famous compendium of childhood terrors and delights, well known for their open and direct approach to cruelty, love, and forgiveness. Bowlby's trilogy is a must; it redefines the field of mental health in the middle of this century, because it completely refocuses child development on direct observation of children, allowing us to formulate testable hypotheses and generate scientific databases and support for our observations regarding the inner life of children. Prior to that, analytic writers were hopelessly caught up in an increasingly idiosyncratic and solipsistic speculation, which in fact led many of them completely to misinterpret dependent behavior in children as pathological. Bowlby showed that attachment and dependence are the building blocks of psychological maturation.

Films also help to refine our clinical skills. *35 and Up* is perhaps the most useful series of recordings of children's lives at different ages, providing us with a unique picture of continuity across time. And Bowlby himself has produced a series of recordings that demonstrate the predictable unfolding of reactions to separation and loss.

What do we encounter in terms of problems? More than we anticipate. The most devastating child psychiatric syndromes make their appearance in this age range: autism and other pervasive developmental disorders, as well as mental retardation in its most severe forms. Sleep problems begin to appear and tax parents and patients alike, but fortunately, they are usually benign and tend to improve with age. Disorders of elimination begin at this age and go on into school age, exacting a large toll on children unless they are properly treated. Disorders of the attachment process are most important to diagnose because they have profound implications for the child's future. Gender issues come to the fore, especially for boys, and they need to be handled sensibly and sensitively. And finally, we see syndromes associated with profound failures of parenting: abuse, neglect, the fabrication of illness in children by their own parents, and problems with feeding, which can lead to lack of growth and even emaciation.

The chapter authors are faculty and staff members of the Division of Child Psychiatry and Child Development at Stanford University. Each, an expert in his or her area, routinely sees a large volume of the cases described, is fully appraised of the research in the field, and has condensed and tailored it to your needs.

ACKNOWLEDGMENTS

As before, many people have helped us in the process of producing this book. Marsha Wallace provided expert editorial assistance, finely honed by her assistance on the previous two volumes. Alan Rinzler once again provided us with detailed editorial help and the opportunity to see this three-volume series come to fruition. Our families and patients deserve our grateful thanks, as do our trainees, who through their persistent questioning force us to do more research and push toward new knowledge.

NOTES

P. xiii, *Intimate attachments to other human beings:* Bowlby, J. (1969). *Attachment and loss.* New York: Basic Books.

P. xiv, *As Daniel Stern's outstanding series of investigations has shown:* Stern, D. (1990). *Diary of a baby.* New York: Basic Books; Stern, D. (1977). *The first relationship: Mother and infant.* Cambridge: Harvard University Press; Stern, D. (1985). *The interpersonal world of the infant: A view from psychoanalysis and developmental psychology.* New York: Basic Books.

P. xv, *The mastery of advanced means . . . opens the world in new and scary ways:* Grimm, J., Grimm, L., & Grimm, K. (1978). *The Brothers Grimm popular folk-tales.* Garden City, NY: Doubleday.

P. xv, *The Brothers Grimm . . . primitive childhood fears on separation from family:* Grimm, J. (1944). *Hansel and Gretel: A story of the forest.* New York: Knopf.

P. xvi, *toddlers simultaneously also create their own "portable parents":* Wise Brown, M. (1947). *Goodnight moon.* New York: Harper & Row.

P. xvi, *Maurice Sendak has captured that moment in children's lives:* Sendak, M. (1963). *Where the wild things are.* New York: Harper& Row.

P. xvi, *We need to be receptive and still, . . . we need to make them feel in charge of the situation:* Fraiberg, S., & Fraiberg, L. (Eds.). (1987). *Selected writings of Selma Fraiberg.* Columbus: Ohio State University Press.

P. xvii, *Books are useful too:* Hoban, R. (1994). *Egg thoughts, and other Frances songs.* New York: HarperCollins; Hoban, R. (1964). *A baby sister for Frances.* New York: Harper & Row; Hoban; R. (1964). *Bread and jam for Frances.* New York: Harper & Row.

P. xvii, *The* Just So *Stories by Rudyard Kipling:* Kipling, R. (1987). *Just so stories for little children.* Harmondsworth: Penguin Books.

P. xvii, *Bowlby's trilogy is a must:* Bowlby, J. (1991). *Attachment and loss.* New York: Penguin Books.

P. xvii, 35 and Up *is perhaps the most useful series of recordings:* Apted, M. (Director/Producer). (1991). *35 and UP.* [Film]. Samuel Goldwyn Co., Academy Entertainment, & Granada Academy Elite.

Für meine Kinder, Remy, Chris, und Josh,
denn sie lehrten mich im tiefsten Sinne

TREATING
PRESCHOOL CHILDREN

GENERAL PRINCIPLES AND TREATMENT

Richard J. Shaw and S. Shirley Feldman

Many factors contribute to the development of psychological and behavioral difficulties seen in infants and children during the preschool-age years. Some infants are predisposed to develop abnormalities due to their genetic makeup. Others are at risk due to exposure to viral infections, such as rubella, or the effects of the maternal use of drugs and alcohol during the pregnancy. The mother's health and nutritional status are also important. Similarly, premature infants are at risk of cognitive and academic delays, and problems with attention. Numerous social and environmental issues may affect their development. For example, families in which there is a high incidence of marital conflict, divorce, alcohol and substance abuse, poverty, or stressful life events are likely to have children with a higher incidence of psychiatric difficulties. In addition, children are at greater risk if their mother is depressed or suffering from a major psychiatric illness.

It is of interest that some factors appear to protect children from developing various psychological disturbances. Some infants appear to be resilient due to high intelligence or adaptability. Parents who are emotionally available and supportive, with a good marital relationship, and families with strong social support and financial resources also appear to foster healthy development. The nature of the child's attachment to the parent, a focus of this chapter, may influence development and subsequent psychological health. Knowledge of both risk and preventive factors may help us intervene to prevent later psychiatric illness.

In this chapter we review three basic issues that are important in the assessment and treatment of preschool-age children: temperament, issues in attachment and separation-individuation, and impulse control. Although these three issues are not unique to the preschool-age child, they appear to take on particular importance in this age group, and problems in these areas frequently result in requests for psychiatric consultation.

TEMPERAMENT

Thirty years ago, the behavioral and psychological disturbances seen in children were presumed to be a result of harmful parenting practices. Clinicians emphasized the central role of the child's environment, even with respect to illnesses such as autism and schizophrenia, which are now known to have a primary biological etiology. Now, however, there is a recognition that a child's biological predisposition to behave and react in a certain style may influence that child's behavior and social relationships. The concept of temperament helps us understand the issues of early childhood and predict a child's subsequent psychiatric and behavioral difficulties.

Although interest in the concept of temperament goes back many years, it was not until the 1950s that two psychiatrists, Alexander Thomas and Stella Chess, helped to establish its importance. Following a series of studies involving interviews of parents and direct observations of infant behavior, Thomas and Chess noted that infants have a biological predisposition to behave with certain characteristic and predictable styles. They used the term *temperament* to describe the phenomenon of how rather than why infants behave with these distinctive styles.

Temperament can be defined as the stable behavioral and emotional reactions that appear early in life and appear to be influenced at least in part by genetic or constitutional factors. Thomas and Chess identified nine dimensions of temperament, which are described in Table 1.1.

Table 1.1
Dimensions of Temperament

Activity Level	The degree of physical activity present in terms of the infant's motor activity during both active and inactive periods of the day.
Rhythmicity	The predictability or unpredictability of the infant's behavior in relation to basic functions such as the sleep-wake cycle, eating, and daily activities.
Approach-Withdrawal	The nature of the infant's initial response to any new stimulus, whether as simple as trying out a new food or something more complex such as meeting a new person or encountering a new situation.
Adaptability	The infant's ability to adapt to a new or altered situation.
Threshold of Response	The intensity level of stimulation necessary to evoke a response in the infant.
Intensity of Reaction	The energy level of the response observed in the infant.
Quality of Mood	The amount of pleasant or positive mood witnessed in the infant.
Distractibility from Tasks or Interests	The ease with which the infant is distracted
Attention Span/ Persistence	The length of time an infant can stay focused on a particular activity and the degree to which the infant stays focused in the face of distraction.

Source: Adapted from Chess, S., & Thomas, A. (1986). Appendix A: Temperamental categories and their definition. In *Temperament in clinical practice*. New York: Guilford. Reproduced with permission.

Classification of Temperament

Thomas and Chess proposed three types of temperament based on a characteristic profile of several of these dimensions—*easy*, *difficult*, or *slow-to-warm-up*—although they recognized that a substantial proportion of the children did not fit into this classification. Nonetheless, longitudinal follow-up of the children they identified as having a specific profile of temperament in infancy suggested that these characteristics persisted over time.

Easy. Easy children, making up 40 percent of Thomas and Chess's original sample, are generally easygoing and delightful babies. They tend to be good-natured and smile frequently. These children respond positively to new experiences and situations, and they quickly establish reliable and predictable routines. They are adaptable and flexible, and generally do well in both school and social situations.

Difficult. Difficult children, making up 10 percent of the original sample, tend to express characteristically negative moods and cry frequently. They are fussy and irritable, and they struggle to adjust to new situations or demands. They tend to have difficulties establishing regular eating and sleeping routines. Their irregular and intense negative responses, combined with slow adaptability, often result in these children having significant difficulties with socialization. Consequently, they are much more likely to be diagnosed with a psychiatric disorder than children with an easy profile of temperament. Parents of children with a difficult temperament often struggle to manage their child's behavior, and they commonly feel guilty and anxious about their parenting skills.

Slow-to-Warm-Up. Children with this temperament profile tend initially to show mildly negative responses to unfamiliar or new situations, but if they are given the opportunity to test out a new situation without pressure, they tend to adapt well. On first impression, these children may appear shy and withdrawn, and it is common for them to be diagnosed as inhibited or insecure. This turns out, however, not to be the case since these children adapt well and establish good social and peer relationships in the right circumstances. Children in this group made up 15 percent of Thomas and Chess's original sample.

Although the classification of temperament that Thomas and Chess proposed is well known and widely used, there have been several more recent classifications, which appear to have some validity. Cloninger, for example, describes the characteristics of harm avoidance, novelty seeking, and dependence on social rewards. Other concepts reported in the literature include introversion and extroversion, emotionality, impulsivity, activity, and sociability.

Goodness of Fit

Children with a difficult temperament profile are at much greater risk of encountering problems as they struggle with the demands of parents and schools, as well as the expectations of society at large. In many cases, these demands may result in an exaggeration of a particular temperamental trait. It may, for example, be unrealistic to expect a physically active child to sit still in a classroom for long periods of time. Similarly, exposing children with a difficult temperament to a host of new activities may result in an exaggerated negative response. In many cases, parents and teachers may misunderstand the "difficult" behavior, and clinicians' failure to appreciate the importance of temperament may lead to inappropriate psychiatric diagnoses.

Thomas and Chess proposed the concept of *goodness of fit* to recognize the importance of the interaction between the child's temperament and the expectations of the environment. Goodness of fit refers to the degree of compatibility between individual temperamental characteristics and the quality of the environment. If there is a good fit between the child's temperament and the personality and expectations of the parents, it is likely that the child's development and adaptation to the environment will proceed smoothly. Since temperament is believed to be primarily biologically determined, one implication is that parents need to modify their expectations and demands to match the temperament of their infants. For example, children who are very physically active and enjoy variety and change are likely as adults to do poorly in a sedentary, mundane office job, but they may excel in an active, outdoor career. Only later does the child develop an increased maturity and ability to modify his or her behavior and adapt to environmental demands.

Adjusting to the difficult child does not imply that the child should be allowed to become a tyrant. Parents and teachers need to strike a balance between excessive demands for conformity versus making no demands at all. Parents need to exercise their ability to help shape the behavior of their child to achieve a positive adaptation to the environment. If parents relinquish control and allow the child to be intimidating just for the purposes of gaining momentary peace and quiet, the child's socialization is derailed, and the child fails to learn appropriate social skills and conduct.

As clinicians, we have a responsibility to promote a goodness of fit between the child and the environment. This may include educating parents, other caretakers, and teachers about methods of adapting to a child with a difficult temperament profile. It is important that parents learn the skills of exercising control and authority, without becoming overzealous, interfering, or domineering in their parenting style, as illustrated in the following case example.

BRAD

Brad, an energetic and social five-year-old, was brought in for an evaluation regarding his distractibility and apparent inability to follow through on tasks. His mother reported that during infancy, Brad had difficulty finishing meals when his attention was distracted. His playroom was always a mess, because he had a tendency to start play-ing with one toy, quickly lose interest in it, and turn his attention to other toys. It was almost impossible to get him to tidy up for simi-lar reasons. Brad's high distractibility remained a problem when he entered school. His inability to follow through on errands and tasks in a timely and systematic way was frustrating to his parents and teachers, and suggested to them that he might have an Attention-Deficit/Hyperactivity Disorder. Psychological testing, however, showed that he was able to focus and complete tasks when he was tested in a quiet, nonstimulating environment. Brad's distractibility was more accurately identified as a temperamental trait, which was likely to be lifelong.

In our clinical work, we focused on educating Brad's parents and teachers on strategies that could maximize his strengths, recogniz-ing that he was likely to require their constant vigilance to help him keep track of his responsibilities and to ensure that there were as few competing distractions as possible when they wanted him to com-plete various tasks.

Temperament in the Preschool-Age Child

Although expectations of children increase during the preschool-age years, children generally welcome these new demands. Chil-dren in this age group start to play with peers in protected social situations and learn the rules of acceptable social behavior, such as sharing toys and managing their aggression. Entry into preschool leads to further demands related to peer interactions.

Children with an easy temperament usually find this a joyous and exciting time, filled with new opportunities and experiences. Their "difficult" counterparts, however, may have an entirely different experience. It may be difficult, for example, for a child with irregular patterns of behavior to adapt to the structure of a preschool. Similarly, the tentative and reserved slow-to-warm-up child is at risk of difficulties in new social groups. In the following case example, we illustrate how the temperamental quality of persistence may lead to school and behavioral difficulties.

CHELSEA

Chelsea was a four-year-old child with great persistence but a somewhat difficult temperament. Her irregular biological rhythms made it difficult for her parents to get her to eat and sleep on a regular schedule. Chelsea's persistence and sociability, however, were seen as strengths by her teachers, who were impressed by her ability to persevere with puzzles and games. Nevertheless, these same qualities of persistence sometimes led to problems; for example, when she was engaged in a certain activity, it was exceedingly difficult to get her to move on to something else without great wails of protest. Chelsea's teachers fortunately had sufficient experience and knew not to overact to these outbursts. A firm yet patient approach helped Chelsea to refocus on new tasks with the same degree of intensity.

As the example illustrates, it is often necessary to educate parents and teachers about the concepts of temperament and goodness of fit to prevent a child from being identified as having psychological difficulties. The clinician's goal in parent guidance is to change the parent's attitudes and behavior to improve the goodness of fit, and in so doing engage the parents as a therapeutic ally. In this way, parent guidance differs from formal psychotherapy, where the goal may be to change the more subtle problems relating to the parent's psychological issues, or maladaptive defense mechanisms. Therapy, however, may be indicated if there is significant psychopathology in the parent or child.

Temperament and School Functioning

Entering school creates further demands and expectations of the child. Parents can play a critical role by preparing their children for this challenging new experience. Many preschools allow parents to bring the child to visit ahead of time and to attend classes with their children until they are ready to be weaned. This practice also provides the opportunity for parents to educate the teachers about particular characteristics of their children.

Temperament can have a strong influence on the child's social and academic functioning. Experienced teachers develop strategies for managing "difficult" behavior. Rather than labeling an active, restless child as hyperactive, the teacher may find it helpful to send the child on regular errands or chores to provide an outlet for motor activity. These children often do better if given the opportunity to learn in short, energetic bursts due to their shorter attention spans. Persistent, nondistractible children, by contrast, quickly apply themselves to work; even here, the teacher needs to exercise caution since too great a focus on work may interfere with the child's social development. In general, it is important to adapt classroom practices wherever possible to foster learning and participation for children with different profiles of temperament.

Temperament and Attention-Deficit/Hyperactivity Disorder

Attention-Deficit/Hyperactivity Disorder is one of the most frequently diagnosed psychiatric disorders in childhood, affecting 5 to 10 percent of the school-age population, primarily boys. Many thousands of children are prescribed stimulant medications to manage impulsive behavior, improve concentration, and reduce motor activity. The classic symptoms of Attention-Deficit/Hyperactivity Disorder, in particular short attention span and high level of physical activity, are also normal variations of temperament. Clinicians need to pay particular attention to this dilemma before rushing to a premature psychiatric diagnosis, which will then lead in most cases to pharmacological treatment. If these behaviors are seen as part of the spectrum of normal temperament, it is just as valid to see the school difficulties as a problem in the goodness of fit between the child and the school environment. Inappropriate diagnosis of a psychiatric disorder may lead in the short term to better control of the behaviors, but it also carries the risk of damage to the child's self-esteem regarding what the child experiences as a core part of his or her identity.

Significance of Difficult Temperament

Numerous studies have supported the original assertion of Thomas and Chess that infants with a difficult temperament profile are more likely to have behavioral problems during adolescence. These children are also more vulnerable to psychiatric disorders in response to stressors, including, for example, psychiatric illness in a parent. Adolescents assessed with difficult temperament also have a higher incidence of childhood behavior problems, which include conduct disorder, substance abuse, delinquent activity, and depression. The task of the clinician is to anticipate these issues and to help parents and teachers develop creative strategies to increase the likelihood of a better outcome for their children.

ATTACHMENT AND
SEPARATION-INDIVIDUATION

One of the major tasks for children during the first three years of life is the development of a secure attachment to their parents. The parent-child bond is so fundamental that it must be considered in the assessment of all childhood disorders. We use the term *attachment* to describe the bond that exists between an infant and the primary caretaker. Although in this chapter we use the term *mother* when discussing issues related to attachment and development, it is important to emphasize that infants are capable of forming attachments to any interested, available figure. In fact, infants develop attachments to multiple figures.

Attachment, the sense of being loved and valued, develops gradually over the first few years and is a key component of human development. The infant's attachment to the mother is the basis of the child's subsequent acceptance of the parents' authority and their socialization efforts. When attachment is proceeding normally, the infant develops a sense of trust that the mother will meet his or her needs. This sense of security permits the infant to venture forth and explore both the inanimate environment and people in his or her social world. Thus, attachment is linked to the child's curiosity, exploration, and cognitive development, on the one hand, and sociability and the emergence of social skills on the other. This attachment or sense of trust is the foundation for the development of self-esteem. Finally, attachment is important for emotional regulation, since the mother's presence provides the attached infant comfort and calming when the child is upset or overwhelmed by excessive stimulation.

The mother's attachment to her infant is also important in that it reduces the chance that she will abuse or neglect her child. Mothers who are securely attached to their infants tolerate the many aversive and difficult situations inherent in parenting, and they develop a sense of satisfaction from their ability to parent their children. This attachment ensures that they will remain involved and invested in the child's well-being for the long haul.

Development of Attachment

Several important biological factors foster the development of attachment. Both infants and mothers have innate reflexes that facilitate attachment behavior. Shortly after birth, infants show a special interest in human faces and eyes, and they soon start to smile on seeing familiar faces. The infant's smile generally promotes predictable reactions in adults, who typically respond by smiling back, talking to the infant in baby talk, or touching or picking up the infant.

Parents become upset by the cries of their infants, and they quickly learn to distinguish cries of hunger, pain, and anger. Crying usually prompts a parent to pick up the infant in order to provide comfort. The fact that the infant can be comforted by being fed or caressed, or even by feeling a parent's heartbeat, leads to feelings of effectiveness in the parent, which also encourages the growth of attachment.

In the second half of the first year, infants make important social changes. In addition to crying and smiling to get attention, they start to vocalize (coo and babble) and to engage in turn taking in vocal exchanges with the mother. At this age, they begin to delight in social games such as peekaboo.

Infants express a strong desire to remain close to their mothers. They show distress when they are separated, and relief and joy when they are reunited. They remain oriented toward their mothers even when they are not with them and will listen for signs of their return. In addition, as soon as they can crawl, infants start to follow their mothers around.

By the age of eight months, infants become cautious and nervous in the presence of strangers, heralding the onset of what has come to be called *stranger anxiety*. Infants tend to seek out their mothers when they feel threatened or afraid. By this age, it is possible to see that the infant has developed a selective preference as well as a strong and relatively enduring emotional tie to the mother. It is this bond that we refer to as the infant's *attachment*.

Why Infants Become Attached

Infants have an inborn need to be close to people and will become attached to the one person who engages in responsive interactions with them over time. For a number of years, researchers thought that feeding was the primary factor that determined the infant's primary attachment. More recent work has shown that the development of attachment is a complex process and that hunger and feeding may be, at best, only minor factors. Parents function in multiple roles, which include providing the pleasure of physical contact, the comfort from being soothed, the opportunity for play, and the first experience of being in a social relationship. Surprisingly, infants also become attached to caretakers who are abusive and punishing.

Because newborn infants have a limited repertoire to express their needs and desires, it is important that the parents anticipate and provide for the basic functions necessary to support life. Through consistent and predictable caretaking, parents create a familiar and secure place for their infants to turn to when threatened or confused by new situations. The infant learns to trust the parent's competence in dealing with his or her needs and in unfamiliar situations that are beyond the infant's comprehension and control.

Another important factor promoting attachment is that of play. Infants quickly learn the pleasure of play with their parents, and they express a preference for spending time with adults who provide this opportunity. Play is often an area in which fathers excel, particularly in arousing, physically energetic games. This is not to imply that mothers are less skillful at playing or that fathers are less able to feed and comfort their infants. Nonetheless, it is possible that social and cultural factors foster different types of relationships with each parent.

Separation Anxiety

Infants aged five to six months typically protest and show distress when separated from their mothers. This separation anxiety reaches a peak at age thirteen months and then declines. The presence of separation anxiety implies that the infant is able to think about and remember the mother in her absence, but cannot understand why she has left and does not know whether she will return. Separation anxiety is a healthy sign in that it indicates that the infant feels attached to the mother. Although the presence of the father or some other familiar figure may help to reduce the intensity of the distress, children do not get used to being separated from their mothers until they have sufficient cognitive abilities to comprehend that she will return.

The wane in the intensity of separation anxiety during the second year of life is a twofold process: the infant comes to know and trust that separations are temporary, and the infant's natural curiosity stimulates a desire to explore the world beyond that of the mother.

In some cases, children traumatized at an early age may develop particular anxieties around the issue of separation, which may lead to the diagnosis of what we term a Separation Anxiety Disorder, illustrated in the following case example.

BRIDGET

Bridget, a five-year-old girl, was brought to her pediatrician for evaluation of symptoms of bed wetting. Bridget had in fact been toilet trained by three years of age, and this current relapse coincided with her entry to school. Bridget's history was significant in that her mother had been hospitalized for treatment of breast cancer when Bridget was only nine months of age. Although Bridget's mother had made an excellent recovery, her illness had resulted in frequent separations from her daughter. In addition, Bridget's mother was particularly withdrawn and depressed at the time of her original diagnosis, and it was necessary for Bridget to be cared for by her grandmother during the initial period of treatment. Further history revealed that Bridget was unable to sleep at night, and her parents had allowed her to start sleeping in their bedroom.

After referral to a child psychiatrist, assessment showed that Bridget's entry to school had brought up profound fears of abandonment, prompted by the separation from her mother. The separation had revived the anxieties she had experienced at the time of her mother's first diagnosis with breast cancer. These anxieties intensified during the initial stage of play therapy, but her bed wetting resolved, and she was able to start sleeping alone at night as she worked through the feelings with her therapist.

Separation-Individuation

In her important infant observation studies, the Hungarian psychiatrist Margaret Mahler helped to delineate the developmental process called *separation-individuation*. Mahler described the sequence of behaviors observed in normal infants as they start to separate psychologically from the state of fusion with the mother, which she termed symbiosis. These stages of development are summarized in Table 1.2.

A child's reliance on the mother becomes less intense during the third and fourth years of life. Opportunities for exposure to new situations combined with increased cognitive skills allow the child to draw on past experience to manage unfamiliar situations. Increased maturity leads children to become more concerned with developing the psychological aspects of their relationships, rather than just maintaining physical proximity.

Mahler's findings have great relevance for the treatment of children and adults. In children with Separation Anxiety Disorder, it is common to find a history of difficulties during the phases of separation-individuation, or a history of significant early losses that have interfered with the child's ability to develop a secure feeling of identity and self-confidence.

Secure and Insecure Attachment

There are considerable differences in the types of attachment that develop in individuals. Research by Mary Ainsworth has led to the development of a classification system for attachment. Based on her observations of infants separated briefly from their mother, Ainsworth derived three types of attachment, which she termed insecure-avoidant (A), securely attached (B), and insecure-resistant (C).

In general, securely attached infants are more confident and independent, and they are more likely to establish social and peer relationships when they are older. They are also better able to

Table 1.2
Margaret Mahler's Stages of Separation-Individuation

Normal Autistic Phase (zero to four weeks)

- The primary task for the infant to accomplish during this phase is that of maintaining homeostasis, or equilibrium with the environment. This implies obtaining the necessary nourishment and protection to allow growth and development.

Normal Symbiotic Phase (four weeks to five months)

- During this phase, the infant is said to be in a state of psychological fusion with the mother. This implies that the infant does not recognize the mother as being a separate person. The infant believes that the mother can be conjured up to gratify needs for food and comfort. She does not exist as a person other than to provide for the infant.

Separation-Individuation: Differentiation (five to ten months)

- The infant starts to develop a sense of being a person separate from the mother and realizes that the mother is a real and separate person.
- The infant shows a growing degree of attachment to the mother, actively seeking her out for comfort and soothing.
- The infant shows the onset of stranger anxiety, meaning that strangers provoke feelings of anxiety and insecurity, which prompt the infant to seek out the mother as a comforting and familiar figure.

communicate using facial expressions, gestures, and vocalizations. Infants assessed as being securely attached at age twelve months seem to interact willingly with friendly strangers and undertake new tasks with enthusiasm. They find it easy to ask for help but are not overly reliant on help. By contrast, infants with an insecure pattern of attachment are less likely to engage in new tasks, give up easily, and tend to avoid unfamiliar adults. Insecure attachment is also associated with subsequent behavior problems, psychological difficulties, and problems with peer relationships.

The first three years of life are particularly important for the development of attachment. There may be a sensitive period between the ages of six and twenty-four months during which the infant's experiences have a particularly strong influence.

Table 1.2 *(continued)*

Separation-Individuation: Practicing (ten to sixteen months)

- The infant starts to explore the world, using the mother as a secure base, but returning to her whenever he or she feels anxious or uncertain. The infant may check back with the mother, either by returning physically or making eye contact for reassurance.
- The infant shows the onset of separation anxiety. The infant becomes distressed when separated from the mother, primarily because he or she can remember the mother as a comforting figure but cannot understand why she is not present and does not know that she will return.

Separation-Individuation: Rapprochement (sixteen to twenty-four months)

- The infant has a greater awareness of feeling separate from the mother, leading to increased feelings of anxiety. The infant struggles with the desire for independence on the one hand yet fears losing the mother altogether if he or she is too independent.
- The infant's struggle to resolve this conflict is associated with characteristic temper tantrums. The term *rapprochement crisis* is given to describe the process by which the infant comes to realize that he or she can establish a feeling of independence while at the same time being able to turn to the parent for support.

Separation-Individuation: Consolidation (twenty-four to thirty-six months)

- The final accomplishment in this process is the development of object constancy. The infant comes to tolerate separations from the mother with the knowledge that she will return. During the mother's absence, the infant is able to maintain an internal image of her as a source of comfort.

However, early attachment patterns do not necessarily become permanent characteristics, and if, for example, the quality of the parenting changes, it is possible to see parallel changes in the child's style of attachments.

Influences on Attachment

A number of maternal and infant characteristics are thought to have an important influence on the nature of the child's attachment. Although both the mother and the child contribute to the attachment relationship, maternal characteristics are generally thought to be the more important.

Maternal Characteristics. Mothers play a crucial role with regard to the development of their child's attachment. Mothers who are slow in responding to their infant's cues or unskilled in terms of their parenting abilities are likely to produce an anxious pattern of attachment in their infant. There are similar findings with parents who are not able to be appropriately affectionate with their infants. Mothers have been classified according to their caregiving style, based on the degree of their sensitivity, consistency, responsiveness, and accessibility and the degree to which they express positive emotions toward their infants, all of which influence the nature of attachment. The dimensions of sensitivity and responsiveness appear to be the most important elements that predict secure attachment.

Infant Characteristics. Certain infants, by virtue of their temperament, appear to be less well disposed to the attempts of their mothers to foster attachment. Infants, for example, who are irritable or restless, and who do not appear to enjoy being cuddled and held, may resist their parents' attempts to bond. These infants may require a great degree of parental persistence and patience. Similar issues may arise with infants who are cognitively delayed or have hearing impairments. In these cases, parents may require help in identifying strategies to foster attachment.

Applications of Attachment Theory to Preschool-Age Children

Knowledge of attachment theory has informed us in a number of important areas that have relevance for the preschool-age child. One example of this is in the area of foster care.

Foster Care. Infants who are placed in foster care between the ages of seven and eighteen months are more likely to show signs of emotional disturbance than infants placed in foster care at a younger age. It is thought that these infants are old enough to have developed a significant attachment to their mothers, but they are unable to understand why the relationship is being broken. A problem with the foster care system is that it is by nature crisis oriented, and social agencies tend to intervene only when the child's health and safety is threatened. Children often remain in foster care for prolonged periods of time, and some undergo multiple placements while attempts are being made to explore the possibility of reunification with the biological parent. This moving around may be at the expense of the child's emotional and developmental needs. As clinicians, it is important that we take an active stance and look at early intervention with families in crisis, sending out caseworkers to provide support before situations reach a critical level. We should also keep in mind the issue of when to recommend permanent removal and adoption, balancing the developmental needs of the child against the likelihood of being able to intervene successfully with the biological family.

In this section we have discussed some of the important issues related to the development of infant attachment. Influenced by temperament, attachment nonetheless develops primarily as a result of the early experiences of the infant in relation to the mother. Patterns of attachment can be identified that have a strong influence on the child's subsequent development, most particularly the child's later social relationships. There is a growing interest in the importance of attachment across the life span with recognition that the experiences during the child's formative years come to influence the pattern of the relationships during adulthood. These patterns ultimately influence the adult's relationships with his or her own children, providing a paradigm to explain how psychological issues and conflicts are transmitted from one generation to the next.

IMPULSE CONTROL

Impulse control is one of the major concerns for parents of preschool-age children. Many referrals in this age group result from parents' concerns about their child's level of aggression and noncompliance and difficulties handling their child's behavior. Deliberate noncompliance on the part of the preschooler is such a part of normal development that we have come to talk of the "terrible twos." This is illustrated in the following case example.

PETER

Peter, a spirited and energetic three-year-old boy, was brought to his pediatrician by his mother, Angela, who was concerned about recent changes in his behavior. Peter was the product of an unplanned pregnancy, born to his mother when she was seventeen years old. Angela, a single mother, had managed well with Peter during his first two years, relying on the services of a day-care center while she worked hard to complete her training as a nursing assistant. She was now concerned about Peter's dramatic behavior change: her pleasant and obliging child had suddenly become prone to explosive temper tantrums. Overnight, mealtimes had become a battleground, with Peter throwing food off his plate and screaming when Angela tried to force him to eat. Peter had also started to kick and bite his mother when she tried to dress him in the mornings.

Angela was relieved to hear that this was a normal and predictable part of Peter's development. She was referred to a parent support class, where she learned some general principles related to parenting young children. She was able to institute a simple behavior modification program, consisting of time-outs in his room and stickers as a reward for socially appropriate behavior. Peter quickly responded to this firm yet warm approach, and although he continued to have periodic temper tantrums, they were neither as intense nor as frequent as before.

Young children by nature tend to be impulsive; they have not developed the cognitive maturity to learn from the lessons of the past. Although adults are able to develop complex and long-term plans, infants by contrast often seem to be at the mercy of their environment. What we hope to see emerging during the preschool-age years is the development of their ability to inhibit and regulate behavior, as well as a capacity for self-control. In general, disruptive behavior during the "terrible twos" is a normal part of development; by contrast, extreme manifestations of defiance or prolonged persistence of this behavior often leads to referrals for psychiatric assessment.

Development of Impulse Control

Toddlers in general have a high level of energy, which they release through physical movement. It is common to see young children struggling with feelings of restlessness, and they appear to benefit from opportunities to run around and expend this excess energy. Preschool teachers realize the value of regular exercise breaks, which allow children to sustain focused attention on organized activities. The development of self-control starts with the ability of the child to inhibit motor movements. In addition, increasing social demands require the child to participate in more organized and coordinated activities.

By the second year of life, toddlers have become increasingly able to control their impulses to act. They start to use past experiences to anticipate the future consequences of their actions. Between the ages of three and five years, they learn to moderate the ways in which they perform physical movements and tasks, and they take a more careful and thoughtful approach to problems. This process evolves in tandem with the child's increased ability to respond to verbal instructions. It is possible that there may be a genetic or biological predisposition to be more active, and the issue of the child's temperament is relevant here in terms of the individual child's degree of impulsiveness.

Problem-Solving Styles

Impulsiveness is evident not only in a child's physical activity and behavior but may be seen in the type of problem-solving strategies used by the child. Young children lack the patience to think about the questions being posed, and they tend to leap to conclusions. They use what has been termed *impulsive* problem solving in contrast to what in adults we describe as *reflective* problem solving. In general, use of an impulsive style indicates that the child is processing information in a superficial manner, which does not promote a thoughtful or careful approach to problems. There is evidence that the tendency to use an impulsive style may be influenced by temperament. Children are more likely to use a reflective style when adults are present to encourage a more considered and thoughtful approach. In addition, increased cognitive development and the process of socialization lead to a general increase in the use of a reflective approach.

Control of Emotions

Young children are easily flooded with new emotions. During the preschool-age years, they learn to inhibit the strong feelings that in infancy lead to feelings of disorganization. Episodes of crying and loss of temper tend to decrease as the child begins to impose his or her own degree of control over feelings of frustration. Girls seem to do a better job of this than boys, who are much more likely to be referred for treatment at this age.

It is not known whether children learn to inhibit their states of emotional arousal or whether they feel just as upset but are better able to conceal their feelings. The task for children is to develop a degree of voluntary control over their emotional states. Unlike other maturational processes, children do not automatically develop the capacity for impulse control. In fact, children who are not socialized and to some degree compelled to show self-restraint are unlikely ever to develop this ability. In these cases, we may see the behavior witnessed in hyperaggressive preadolescent boys, who are unable to tolerate frustration or develop the ability to plan and think ahead.

Delaying Gratification

Implicit in the ability to control impulses for action is the ability to delay gratification. The child needs to learn to appreciate that it is possible both to experience feelings of frustration and know that there may be a reward at a later date. Younger children may have particular difficulties with this concept, since their level of cognitive development does not allow them to keep in mind the possibility of future events. Between the ages of five and twelve, however, children are increasingly able to hold their impulses in check. In addition, they may be able to forgo an immediate small reward for the prospect of a larger one in the future. The ability to delay gratification depends both on how long the wait is and whether the child believes that there is a reward to wait for. Younger children in particular do not have the full repertoire of strategies for distraction necessary to reduce the feelings of frustration during the waiting period.

The Parents' Role in Children's Impulsiveness

All young children are impulsive during their early years. A parent's task is to create an environment in which children are able to act safely on their impulses. At the same time, parents need to take on regulating functions on behalf of their children, until they are sufficiently mature to do this themselves. These tasks include helping with planning and organization for the basic daily activities of eating, sleeping, and play. Children have a limited ability to plan, and parents function initially as the child's memory. Parents make choices on behalf of their children and also take responsibility for the consequences of these decisions. Parents act as role models, fostering the development of self-control. In essence, they provide the external structure that is both helpful and necessary for their child's development.

Parents take on many other roles in teaching their children about the importance of impulse control. As their children get older, parents provide increasing opportunities for their children to share in decision making. At times, this may include allowing the child to make decisions that are not necessarily the best ones. Nonetheless, a child who is given the opportunity to experience the consequences of both good and bad decisions may learn from mistakes. Parents must also provide the opportunity for thoughtful choices and for children to experience the consequences of their decisions. Children acquire self-control not simply by getting older but through a learning process. Parents may have to step in and set limits to protect a child, and provided that this is done in a respectful and empathic manner, these limits will be both reassuring and helpful to the child.

Hyperactive children are particularly in need of structure. They quickly lose interest in things, and do not have the frustration tolerance to wait for activities to begin. Frequently they have to be told what to do next, and they may not do well in a very unstructured home or school environment. Parents need to keep these factors in mind when they make choices about potential school settings for their child.

Parents have a responsibility to prove that they are trustworthy over time. Often a child's emotional outbursts may strain the parents' capacity for self-control, particularly if they have not outgrown their own impulsiveness. Parents who are inexperienced, depressed, or overwhelmed may similarly have difficulties with younger children. Parents in conflict with each other or who disagree with each other about child-rearing practices may also have children who exhibit problems with self-control. These problems are likely to persist through childhood into adolescence.

∿

The remainder of this book is devoted to the common clinical disorders seen in infants and preschool-age children. In many cases, these disorders have their origin in or are amplified by derailment in one of the three areas discussed in this chapter. For example, our understanding of Attention-Deficit/Hyperactivity Disorder is enhanced by considering the importance of both temperament and problems with impulse control. Sleep disturbances and feeding disorders may have their origins in the failure to develop secure attachment, and abuse and neglect may result in disorders of both attachment and impulse control. Separation Anxiety Disorder and disorders of attachment may reflect not only the issues of attachment, but also those of individual differences in temperament; for example, the temperamentally restrained and inhibited child may be at much greater risk of developing a Separation Anxiety Disorder in contrast to active children who are constantly seeking out new experiences.

For a child to flourish, there must be a good match between the child's temperament and his or her environment, especially the parenting environment. Certainly parents and schoolteachers need to accommodate to the needs of the child, but it is equally important for the child to learn to accommodate to the environment, particularly when it comes to impulse control. These early interactions between parents and children lay the groundwork for all subsequent development, and they affect the child's receptiveness to subsequent socialization. Knowledge of these concepts will help guide and inform treatment interventions.

FOR FURTHER READING

Ainsworth, M. D. (1964). Patterns of attachment behavior shown by the infant in interaction with his mother. *Merrill-Palmer Quarterly, 10*, 51–58.

Chess, S., & Thomas, A. (1986). *Temperament in clinical practice.* New York: Guilford.

Cloninger, C. R. (1986). A unified biosocial theory of personality and its role in the development of anxiety states. *Psychiatric Development, 4*, 167–226.

Cole, M., & Cole, S. R. (1993). *The development of children* (2nd ed.). New York: Scientific American Books.

Maccoby, E. E. (1980). *Psychological growth and the parent-child relationship.* New York: Harcourt Brace Jovanovich.

Mahler, M. S., Pine, F., & Bergman, A. (1975). *The psychological birth of the human infant.* New York: Basic Books.

Thomas, A., & Chess, S. (1977). *Temperament and development.* New York: Brunner/Mazel.

Zigler, E. F., & Stevenson, M. F. (1993). *Children in a changing world: Development and social issues* (2nd ed.). Pacific Grove, CA: Brooks/Cole.

2

AUTISM, PERVASIVE DEVELOPMENTAL DISORDERS, AND ASPERGER

Linda J. Lotspeich

JUSTIN

Justin, an attractive three-year-old boy, was brought to our clinic by his parents for assessment because he was slow to develop speech. His parents had been concerned about his lack of language since he was twenty-four months old. They were perplexed because he seemed intelligent and enjoyed solving five- to ten-piece jigsaw puzzles, yet he would not speak. They reported that in just the past few months he had begun to imitate the phrases from his favorite videotape, *Thomas the Tank Engine*, exactly mimicking the voice and cadence of each character. He did not use these phrases for communication, but apparently simply for his own enjoyment. Also, he occasionally said "juice" to request a drink, but only when his parents prompted him. When he wanted an object that he could not get on his own, he would take his mother's hand and lead her to it.

Justin had no interest in playing with other children and would run away if a child approached. He interacted with his parents only when they initiated the interaction; nonetheless, they reported that he was very affectionate. He never brought toys or preschool projects to his parents for social display. He played almost exclusively with toy trains. He had several sets, and he liked to line up the cars and move them around a circular track. Sometimes he would look at his trains while flapping his hands. At other times he would put his head down on the floor while moving his trains, to watch the wheels turn, and he would play like this for hours. Justin had frequent temper tantrums, especially when taken outside his home, for instance, to a neighborhood shop or restaurant; as a consequence his parents avoided taking him into the community.

During my assessment, I evaluated Justin's play and behavior, and my associate gave him a variety of psychological tests. When he was introduced to me, he did not smile or meet my gaze. A preschool developmental test measured his expressive and receptive language at the twelve- to eighteen-month level. His visual-perceptual and visual-motor skills, by contrast, were at the thirty-six-month level. During play, he ignored our overtures and either screamed or, when allowed, spent the entire session playing with a toy train he had brought from home. Physical examination revealed nothing unremarkable.

As a result of our evaluation, he was given the diagnosis of Autistic Disorder, and our treatment recommendations included parent education, a behaviorally based special education program, speech and language therapy, and consultation with behavior modification specialists to develop a program aimed at decreasing the frequency of his temper tantrums. We advised Justin's parents that his disorder was not caused by anything they had done, but was a neurological condition. We referred Justin to a pediatric neurologist to determine if he had any known neurological disorders associated with autism.

❧

Autism was first recognized as a distinct syndrome in the early 1940s, when Dr. Leo Kanner, an American psychiatrist, published his now-classic paper describing a group of autistic children. His description is as accurate now as it was then. These children tend to ignore the social overtures of others and prefer to play by themselves. Their communication deficits include delayed development of language and inappropriate use of language; many children with autism are mute, and those who do develop language have characteristic impairments in the appropriate communicative use of language. Typically, the interests of these children are repetitive and unusual; they may, for instance, be fascinated by lining up toy cars or by staring at spinning wheels. Some develop inflexible rituals, such as insisting on wearing the same colored shirt each day or eating only pureed foods. Many autistic children test within the mentally retarded range, while others have average and above-average IQs.

Over the twenty years I have worked with autistic children, I have seen a continuing evolution in the diagnostic labels given to these children. Clinicians have increasingly recognized a group of children with symptoms similar to but less severe than those seen in the classically autistic children Kanner described. In an attempt to distinguish these less impaired children, new diagnostic terms have come into the autism literature, and others have disappeared. Currently the practice is to place both autism and the less severe forms of it under the umbrella category of Pervasive Developmental Disorders (PDD). The term reflects the pervasive nature of these impairments, emphasizing that the children have deficits in many areas of development: socialization, communication, play, and routines. In addition, the term denotes that these are disorders of early childhood development.

PDD is defined in the *DSM-IV* as a diagnostic category that encompasses five disorders (see Table 2.1). The three most common of these are autism, Pervasive Developmental Disorder–Not Otherwise Specified (PDD-NOS), and Asperger's Disorder. The remaining two, Rett's Disorder and Childhood Disintegrative Disorder, are uncommon.

In this chapter when I use the term *PDD* I am referring inclusively to autistic disorder and to the four other PDD diagnoses. When I use the terms *autistic* or *autism* I am referring only to Autistic Disorder.

Table 2.1
***DSM-IV* Pervasive Developmental Disorders**

Autistic Disorder
Asperger's Disorder
Rett's Disorder
Childhood Disintegrative Disorder
Pervasive Developmental Disorder–Not Otherwise Specified

DIAGNOSIS

Over the years, the diagnostic criteria for autism and the other PDDs have changed to reflect a better understanding of these disorders. Inevitably, new research findings will force additional changes in diagnostic criteria. At present, I often find it difficult to differentiate between partially overlapping PDDs, such as autism and Asperger's Disorder, because there is room for subjective interpretation in assigning diagnostic criteria to an individual. Also, many of the twelve *DSM-IV* diagnostic criteria for autism are used in diagnosing the other forms of PDDs, which adds to the confusion. In this section of the chapter, I first review the diagnostic criteria for autism and then refer back to some of these criteria when discussing the diagnosis of the other PDDs.

Autism

The twelve *DSM-IV* diagnostic criteria for autism are divided into three areas: (1) qualitative impairments in reciprocal social interaction, (2) qualitative impairments in communication, and (3) restricted, repetitive, and stereotyped patterns of behavior, interests, and activities. For a child to be diagnosed with autism, he or she must exhibit at least six of these criteria; at least two criteria must be met in the area of social impairments and at least one in each of the other two areas; and the child must have a history of delay in socialization, communication, or imaginative play prior to the age of thirty-six months.

Qualitative Impairments in Social Interaction. It is often not a simple matter to determine whether a child or adult has a social impairment because the range of social skills in a population of normal children is so broad. Some of us are social butterflies, while others are very shy, avoid eye contact, and are unlikely to initiate a social exchange unless we know the other person well. For most children with autism, however, social deficits are marked, and they go well beyond those seen in the general population in both number and severity. Thus, although observers may differ on a child's score for a single criterion, the number and severity of impairments seen in autism makes the diagnosis fairly clear.

Children with autism typically do not have a range of facial expressions; their facial features appear flat. Compared to other children at their developmental level, they have problems interacting socially with peers and frequently prefer solitary activities. They do not share their interests and pleasures with others. For example, parents frequently report to me that on coming home from school, their child will not spontaneously show them his or her school work. Instead, the parent will find these items in the child's backpack. When they are brought to the attention of the child, the child shows little, if any, interest. Socially, these children are poorly engaged with others and tend to ignore even close relatives.

Qualitative Impairments in Communication. Language delay is the most common reason parents bring their child for an evaluation. For example, parents complain, "My child is only speaking a few single words." Unlike a child who is deaf, children with autism do not naturally use gestures to communicate. Commonly, they let their parent know they are hungry by taking the parent's hand and leading him or her to the refrigerator. Sometimes children with autism use the parent's hand as though it were a tool—for instance, using the parent's finger to point out pictures in a book instead of pointing with their own finger. Those children who are able to speak in sentences typically are unable to engage in true to-and-fro conversations; they either monopolize the conversation or stop talking as soon as the other person fails to prompt them with another question.

Children with autism often echo words and sentences they have heard in television commercials, on favorite videotapes, or from familiar adults. In this type of imitation, known as echolalia, the child typically reproduces the exact tone and cadence of the phrase. Another example of atypical language is pronoun reversal, in which the child refers to himself or herself as *you*, saying, for instance, "You want a cookie" but meaning, "I want a cookie." Pretend play is closely related to the child's language development; in general, children with autism rarely engage in pretend play, such as feeding a doll or talking for an action figure. Autistic preschool children may have difficulty in playing simple interactive games such as peekaboo, pat-a-cake, and ring around the rosie. Generally children with autism not only have language delay, but the language development that does occur is atypical.

Restricted, Repetitive, and Stereotyped Patterns of Behavior, Interests, and Activities.
Restricted and repetitive behaviors are the symptoms that most often allow us to differentiate between autism and a primary language disorder. Autism, however, is not the only medical condition in which restricted and repetitive behaviors are observed. Similar symptoms are also seen, for example, in children with mental retardation and childhood Obsessive-Compulsive Disorder (OCD).

The play of autistic children tends to be extremely focused, to the exclusion of other activities. Common styles of restricted play include activities with trains or other transportation toys, a fixation on numbers and letters (for example, a fascination with commercial logos), and pouring over store catalogs. They may also engage in play that appears nonproductive, such as running back and forth flapping their hands, perseveringly spinning the wheel of a toy car, or lining up objects. These activities are frequently referred to as self-stimulation, meaning that the children appear to find an intense sense of internal satisfaction from these repetitive actions.

In addition to unusual patterns of play, children with autism often insist that their environment and schedule follow a set routine. For example, a child may insist that each time the family goes to the grocery store, they must enter through the same door; if this rule is not followed, the child will frequently have a temper tantrum in the parking lot. To avoid these outbursts, families have learned to incorporate the child's rigid rules into their own daily lives. The character Raymond in the movie *Rain Man* is an autistic man who has many rigid routines; he rearranges the hotel furniture to match the arrangement in his own room at home, and he insists on watching a specific television show at a set time, even though he and his brother are driving through a remote rural area.

PDD-NOS

Children with PDD-NOS have many of the symptoms seen in those with autistic disorder. The distinguishing difference is that the PDD-NOS child exhibits fewer than six of the twelve *DSM-IV* diagnostic criteria for autism. Typically such children have less severe deficits in socialization, but they are likely to have abnormalities in speech and language, such as echolalia. They may or may not have unusual patterns of play or interests. Prior to the 1980s, many of these children were given a diagnosis of language delay; now we recognize that, like children with autism, they too have problems engaging in authentic social interactions and often have unusual interests as well. I find that differentiating between autistic disorder and PDD-NOS is problematic, and in the final analysis the diagnosis is a clinical judgment of the diagnostician. A child with PDD-NOS can have a normal IQ or an IQ within the mental retardation range. Melissa, a preschool child recently evaluated in our clinic, is an example of a child with PDD-NOS.

MELISSA

Melissa, age four, was brought to our clinic by her parents. They had a long list of concerns about their daughter, including her poor attention span, inability to follow adult direction, inappropriate behaviors (spitting), poor peer relations, and language delay. Her parents were first concerned when she was not speaking any words between eighteen and twenty-four months of age. At twenty-four months, she said her first word, followed by two- to three-word phrases at forty-two months. At the time of the evaluation, she spoke in simple phrases and short sentences. She used these phrases to ask for things but still would take the hand of a parent to lead the parent to an object she wanted. Some of her phrases were identical to those her mother used; for example, Melissa would announce "What's the problem?" when she was upset.

Sometimes Melissa tended to tune people out, but she could be very social and brought toys and objects to show to her parents. She was interested in other children and would play next to them but did not play interactively. She was very active, getting into everything, such as emptying drawers, and she was fascinated with long, flexible objects like tape measures, strings, jump ropes, and hoses. She could play all day with these items and would scream and throw a tantrum if they were removed. Sometimes she would pretend that the jump rope was a hose. Melissa's parents had tried to place her in several preschools, but she had extreme difficulty with separation, crying for hours with no indication that she might eventually stop.

On the day of our assessment, Melissa initiated an interaction with me, but she had difficulty sustaining our social interaction. She had adequate eye contact and an appropriate social smile. On testing by my associate, her expressive language was found to be at the thirty-month level and her receptive language at the thirty-six-month level. Her visual-motor and visual-perceptual skills tested at the forty-eight-month level, the same as her chronological age. She met a few of the *DSM-IV* criteria for autism, such as failure to develop appropriate peer relations, delay in spoken language with no compensation through gestures, stereotypic language, and preoccupation with unusual interests or objects.

Because she did not satisfy the full criteria for autism, we diagnosed Melissa with PDD-NOS and recommended a communication-handicapped classroom to improve her language delays and peer communication. We also recommended behavior modification therapy to lessen her inappropriate behaviors (spitting) and her hyperactivity and inattention.

Asperger's Disorder

Asperger's Disorder was first described in the 1940s when Dr. Hans Asperger, a Viennese physician, wrote a paper describing four children who had symptoms similar to but milder than those seen in children with autism. Little clinical notice was taken of this milder disorder until the 1980s, when Dr. Lorna Wing, an autism researcher in England, used the term *Asperger's Syndrome* to describe a group of children she had evaluated. She reviewed Asperger's 1944 paper and noted that many of her patients had a pattern of deficits similar to the group described forty years previously. Since Dr. Wing's report, there has been a resurgence of interest in Asperger's Disorder, as witnessed by numerous recent studies attempting to draw dividing lines between Asperger's Disorder, autism, and PDD-NOS.

Asperger's Disorder first appeared in the *Diagnostic Statistical Manual* in 1994, with the publication of the *DSM-IV*. Thus, the term has been in general use only for a few years. As defined in the *DSM-IV,* Asperger's Disorder is diagnosed when a child demonstrates social impairments and a restricted pattern of interests and routines much like a child with autistic disorder but to a lesser degree. Children with Asperger's Disorder, however, do not have the significant language delay characteristic of children with autism. Despite their relatively normal use of language, I have observed that these children frequently have difficulties engaging in reciprocal conversations. They tend to interact superficially, in general they have difficulties reading social cues, and their social use of language is awkward. Also, by definition, children with Asperger's Disorder have normal cognitive abilities, while approximately 75 percent of children with Autistic Disorder have impaired cognitive abilities, testing in the mentally retarded range.

In my experience, children with Asperger's Disorder are typically brought to my clinic when they are in the early elementary school years. Parents are often concerned about behavioral disturbances rather than with the delayed development more typical of autism and PDD-NOS. Roberto, who came to my clinic when he was seven and a half years old, is an example of such a child.

ROBERTO

Roberto's parents were concerned about his inability to play normally with children his age. They reported that he got into arguments and recently had hit another child during an argument. He had a history of difficulty in play with his peers since his preschool days, though this was the first time he had hit another child. "He seems to want to play with other children," his parents reported, "but he doesn't know how." In fact, he much preferred the company of adults. He had no friends, and so his parents had involved him in organized and prearranged activities, like Little League. Roberto's parents remarked that he seemed very rule-bound. At Little League practice, he liked to lecture and correct the other children on the rules of baseball; in fact, the hitting episode occurred during one of these lectures.

Roberto tended to be a serious child; he was concrete and could not understand jokes that required a leap of insight or had a double meaning. His language development was normal, yet he could not really engage in a normal two-way conversation, and he tended to monopolize the conversation by expounding on his own specific interest. He stopped conversing when other topics were introduced. At the age of two, he had a map of the United States and in fact had memorized all fifty state names at that time. At the time of our evaluation, his exclusive interest was animals, especially exotic or zoo animals. He liked to memorize facts about them and could discuss the difference between an ibex and a wildebeest. He was in a regular second-grade classroom and was at the top of his class in reading and low average in math.

During our assessment, he was administered a test of general intelligence, the Wechsler Intelligence Scale for Children, Third Edition (WISC-III). His verbal IQ was 119, and his performance IQ was 82, resulting in a full-scale score of 98. During the play session, he readily engaged with me in playing with toy animals, but he resisted taking part in pretend play with the animals. Instead, he insisted on talking about the animals themselves: their names, their habits, and where they lived. He seemed quite egocentric because he would not or could not follow my lead in moving through the various activities of the evaluation.

We gave Roberto the diagnosis of Asperger's Disorder. We told his parents that his apparent egocentricity, emphasis on rules, and restricted interest were a consequence of the way his brain processed information. Since social situations with his peers were by nature spontaneous and could not be anticipated, he was more comfortable with adults, who are more predictable and tolerant. To help him improve his interactions with his peers, we recommended speech and language therapy to develop his social use of language and a social skills group for children with Asperger's Disorder.

Rett's Disorder and Childhood Disintegrative Disorder

These two disorders are rare and relatively easy to distinguish from the other PDD diagnoses. Rett's Disorder occurs only in girls and has a characteristic onset. These infants are normal until sometime between five and forty-eight months, when their head circumference decreases. Also, at about this time, they lose purposeful use of their hands and develop a stereotyped wringing movement of their hands. Like children with autism, those with Rett's Disorder also exhibit difficulties in socialization and communication.

Children with Childhood Disintegrative Disorder develop normally during at least the first twenty-four months of life. Sometime later, these children lose previously acquired skills such as language skills. At the same time, they begin to exhibit impairments in socialization, communication, and restricted patterns of play and activities like children with autism. What distinguishes these children from autistic children is that autistic children typically have impairments prior to twenty-four months; it is rare for autistic children to lose previously acquired skills except for the loss of spoken words under the age of twenty-four to thirty months.

ASSOCIATED DISORDERS AND PROBLEMATIC SYMPTOMS

Many children with PDD have additional disorders, which tend to be cognitive impairments, such as mental retardation and learning disabilities. In addition, children with PDD frequently have problematic symptoms that do not appear in the list of twelve diagnostic criteria. These symptoms include aggressive outbursts and hyperactivity.

Mental Retardation

Mental retardation is a disorder of impaired cognition (as measured by IQ testing) and impaired adaptive skills in daily activities (for example, an inability to prepare simple foods). Approximately 75 percent of children with Autistic Disorder also test within the mentally retarded range—usually in the range of mild to moderate, and less often in the range of severe mental retardation. Some children with PDD-NOS have mental retardation, but children with Asperger's Disorder by definition do not have mental retardation.

The term *high-functioning autism* is typically used for children whose Autistic Disorder is accompanied by a normal or above-normal IQ. In contrast, the term *low-functioning autism* is generally applied to children with autism plus mental retardation.

Learning Disabilities

Learning disabilities are a group of disabilities affecting the child's performance in just one area of cognition, for instance, dyslexia, which is a learning disability of reading. Many children with PDD who test within the normal range of intelligence have learning disabilities. This is particularly true for children with PDD-NOS and Asperger's Disorder. Almost any type of learning disability may be seen in a child with PDD-NOS and Asperger's Disorder. One type of learning disability frequently associated with Asperger's Disorder is nonverbal learning disability. Children with a nonverbal learning disability have strengths in verbal skills and weaknesses in visual skills.

Problematic Symptoms

In the clinic I have found that the primary concern of most parents of autistic children, after communication and cognitive deficits are taken into account, is behavior problems. These behavior problems are not unique to PDD, but they are often pronounced and can seriously interfere with the child's progress and the family's peace. The most disturbing behavior problem is aggressive outbursts. As a child psychiatrist, I am frequently asked to evaluate a child for medication treatment for aggressive behaviors. These outbursts, which resemble typical infantile temper tantrums, have many causes, including frustration (stemming from the child's inability to communicate), an inability to shift from one activity to another, and an inability to understand and follow instructions. Another significant behavior problem is self-injurious behaviors, as when a child bites himself or hits his own head. It is unusual for children with these behaviors to injure themselves seriously, but they can cause abrasions, and more serious injuries are possible.

In addition to tantrums and self-injurious behaviors, many children with PDD have a short attention span, hyperactivity, and impulsive behaviors. According to the nomenclature of the *DSM-IV,* these behaviors are part of the child's PDD and are not considered diagnostic of Attention-Deficit/Hyperactivity Disorder (ADHD), despite the similarities in symptoms. Finally, parents regularly complain that their child with PDD does not fall asleep until after midnight or that the child wakes up frequently throughout the night. Insomnia affects the whole family; when the autistic child does not sleep, the parents and siblings frequently do not sleep either.

DIFFERENTIAL DIAGNOSIS

Many of the symptoms of PDD are also seen in other childhood disorders. Disorders of mental retardation and learning disabilities, both associated with PDD, also occur independent of PDD and so need to be differentiated from it. Other disorders that are confused with PDD are language disorders, sensory impairments (visual and hearing), childhood schizophrenia, and OCD.

Mental Retardation and Learning Disabilities

Frequently children with PDD also have mental retardation or a learning disability. It is also common for a child with mental retardation to have a few PDD symptoms without meriting a diagnosis of PDD. For instance, children with profound or severe mental retardation may demonstrate one or more autistic symptoms, such as perseverative play and poor eye contact. However, a child with severe or profound mental retardation typically functions at a developmental age of twenty-four months or younger. In these cases, it is assumed that the "PDD symptoms" are simply congruent with the child's low developmental age and are not due to PDD. In general, the *DSM-IV* PDD criteria are measured against the child's developmental age to determine whether the child has PDD.

Some children with primary learning disabilities have problems with communication and consequently with socialization, but not to the degree seen in children with PDD. Also, children with learning disabilities do not have unusual interests or routines.

Language Disorders

Most children with a PDD have language delays, but not all children with language delays have a PDD. Differentiating between the two is not difficult. Children with language delays do not have unusual play and ritualistic routines. Also, they seldom have atypical forms of communication, such as echolalia, pronoun reversal, or perseverative statements. In most types of language disorders, the child is able to compensate through gestures and elaborate facial expressions; children with a PDD are unable to compensate in this way.

Hearing and Visual Impairments

During their early childhood, children with hearing or vision problems frequently have difficulties in communication and socialization. Visually impaired children sometimes develop stereotyped behaviors, such as wiggling their fingers in front of their eyes. These behaviors are commonly referred to as "blindisms" and should not be confused with autistic behaviors. Children with severe hearing impairments typically compensate by using gestures and facial expressions like those seen in children with primary language disorders; these gestures and expressions are not seen in children with a PDD. For example, it is unusual to encounter a deaf child with poor eye contact. These children typically capitalize on eye contact to communicate more effectively with others. Of course, some children with either a hearing impairment or a visual impairment also have autism or PDD-NOS; this happens only rarely, and when it does, both diagnoses are given.

Childhood Schizophrenia

Childhood schizophrenia typically presents with symptoms of hallucinations, delusions, and social withdrawal. This disorder is only infrequently confused with the PDD, in part because childhood schizophrenia usually presents after the age of five, while the PDDs usually present before the age of three. In addition, childhood schizophrenia is not accompanied by developmental delays like those seen in PDD. Also, PDD children do not have hallucinations or delusions. Asperger's Disorder and childhood schizophrenia are sometimes confused because both are characterized by symptoms of social withdrawal in the absence of severe developmental delays. Hallucinations and delusions, however, are not characteristic of Asperger's Disorder.

Obsessive-Compulsive Disorder

OCD is a disorder of both compulsive behaviors and obsessive thoughts. Compulsive behaviors are nonfunctional behaviors such as excessive hand washing or repetitive checking of door locks. These compulsive behaviors are frequently associated with obsessive, worried thoughts. There is some overlap between the types of compulsions seen in OCD and the types seen in PDD. For example, ritual rearrangement of objects on a table is observed in both disorders. However, children with PDD rarely develop washing rituals. Moreover, children with OCD do not typically have a history of developmental delays. Additionally, most children with OCD have normal social skills, which is not the case in children with any type of PDD. The PDD diagnosis most likely to be confused with childhood OCD is Asperger's Disorder.

EPIDEMIOLOGY

The prevalence of Autistic Disorder is approximately four per ten thousand, a figure that has remained constant through multiple studies and over many years. The prevalence of Rett's Disorder and Childhood Disintegrative Disorder is not known with certainty. These disorders are considered rare, and their prevalence is certainly less than that of Autistic Disorder. The prevalence of PDD-NOS and Asperger's Disorder is also not accurately known, due to a lack of studies and diagnostic uncertainties. Estimates are that the incidence of all the PDDs combined is about ten to fifteen per ten thousand, or possibly higher.

Autism is seen in boys approximately four times more often than in girls. A high ratio of affected males to females is also found for both PDD-NOS and Asperger's Disorder. Rett's Disorder, in contrast, occurs only in females. The gender ratio for Childhood Disintegrative Disorder is unknown.

ETIOLOGY

In the early 1970s, when I was beginning a career as a teacher of developmentally delayed children, there was a passionate debate taking place over the probable causes of autism. At that time, most professionals believed that autism was an emotional disorder caused by poor parenting; others, however, were convinced that autism was a brain disorder caused by a neurologic impairment. The controversy is now settled, and it is universally accepted that autism is not produced by traumatic emotional events. Instead, a variety of data strongly indicate that both autism and the other PDDs are disorders of brain development.

In the majority of cases, the specific brain impairment producing PDD cannot be specified. A number of well-characterized neurological disorders have been associated with a minority of cases of PDD (see Table 2.2). Some of these appear to be genetic in origin. For example, Fragile X Syndrome is seen in about 1 to 3 percent of children with PDD. Fragile X Syndrome is a genetic disorder commonly associated with mental retardation. Tuberous Sclerosis, another genetic disorder, is also strongly associated with PDD. Tuberous Sclerosis is a rare autosomal-dominant syndrome with a wide variety of clinical findings, usually including mental deficiency, seizures, skin lesions, and intracranial nodules.

Neurofibromatosis also has a genetic basis and is characterized by nodules found under the skin and in other organs, including the brain. It is sometimes associated with PDD. Chromosomal Abnormalities exist in many forms. When part of a chromosome is either deleted or duplicated inappropriately, there is an increased risk of abnormal brain development, which may predispose the individual to PDD. Finally, Phenylketonuria, a metabolic disorder with a genetic etiology, may also be associated with PDD if left untreated. In this disorder, lack of a critical enzyme causes an amino acid to build up to toxic levels in both the brain and other organs.

Nongenetic disorders have also been associated with PDD; examples include congenital rubella and several other congenital infections of the brain.

The neurobiological origins for most cases of PDD remain unknown. Research today is focusing on genetic, viral, and autoimmune etiologies; it is also possible that PDD is produced by some combination of these factors. We can anticipate that these studies will lead to the discovery of an increasing number of specific neurological causes of PDD.

Based on family studies, it appears that some forms of PDD are caused by yet unknown genetic disorders. A number of families, many more than would be expected by chance alone, have two or more siblings with PDD. Twin studies have revealed that the concordance for autism in identical twins is much higher than the concordance in fraternal twins. Both observations suggest a genetic etiology for autism, and genetic approaches are being vigorously pursued in autism research.

Table 2.2
PDD-Associated Neurological Disorders

Fragile X Syndrome
Tuberous Sclerosis
Neurofibromatosis
Chromosomal Abnormalities
Phenylketonuria
Congenital Rubella

INITIAL ASSESSMENT

There are many essential elements in the assessment of a child with a possible PDD. An extensive evaluation is required to provide answers to such questions as these:

1. What is the correct specific diagnosis?
2. What is the child's developmental level?
3. Can the cause of the disorder be identified?
4. What treatments are most appropriate?
5. What are realistic expectations for the child's prognosis?

A child's PDD may be identified and diagnosed by a pediatrician, a psychologist, or another professional. However, an evaluation by a clinician from a single discipline is usually not comprehensive enough to answer all of these questions adequately. A full assessment requires a multidisciplinary approach, often by a team of professionals working together. When this is impractical, the parents may arrange serial assessments by various professionals to cover the key elements of the evaluation.

I believe that, whenever possible, professionals with a reputation for conducting comprehensive evaluations on children with PDD should be chosen for these assessments. One reason is that parents will have many questions regarding what is known about the current research, nontraditional medical treatments, most up-to-date educational and behavioral treatments, and current trends in psychopharmacology. Unless the professional has seen many children with PDD and has kept up with trends in both traditional and nontraditional treatments, the parents leave these assessments with many questions unanswered. It is revealing that parents of PDD children who plan to move first determine who the PDD professionals are in that community before making the move.

History

As in any other assessment, the social and medical history is very important. From this history, the clinician learns what the child is like in a variety of settings, such as in the home, at school, and in the community. The interviewer should take a comprehensive history to learn about the child's development and behavior in the areas of communication (verbal and nonverbal), socialization (with adults and peers), play, interests, and routines. Determining age of onset is an important aspect of the history, as it is used to differentiate Childhood Disintegrative Disorder from the other PDDs. Medical histories may also be positive for Seizure Disorder, which is associated with autism. Although autism has a prevalence of only four in ten thousand, approximately 3 percent of children with autism have a sibling with the disorder. When there are close relatives with PDD or other developmental disorders, a detailed family history may support the possibility of a genetic origin for the PDD. When the family history is positive for PDD, the child should be evaluated by a pediatric geneticist.

Behavioral Observations

The behavioral part of the assessment can be done in a variety of settings—the school, the home, the clinic—but most observations are done in a clinical setting: a playroom, an office, or a physical examination room. I prefer to observe the child's play in a playroom with only a few toys, to minimize the possibility of the child's becoming overstimulated, which is all too likely in children with PDD. In the clinic, we initially observe the child in solitary play to assess the style of play; frequently play is repetitive and nonfunctional, such as a lining up all the toy cars. Following this, we intervene and attempt to engage the child in reciprocal play. Children with PDD tend to avoid the overtures of the evaluator or merely follow the lead of the adults; they virtually never initiate reciprocal play.

During the play session, the evaluator also assesses the child's level of pretend play by setting up a scene and inviting the child to play. With older and less impaired children, we also attempt to engage them in a conversation to assess their ability to converse reciprocally on a variety of topics. Children with PDD usually react by talking only about their own specific interest, or they become silent unless the adult structures the conversation by asking additional questions.

It is also important to observe the child's behavior during more structured activities, such as during developmental testing. Many times the children's behavior looks less impaired during testing than in solitary play, because the structure helps to organize their thoughts and behavior.

Developmental Testing

Developmental testing is usually done by a child psychologist trained in the administration of standardized psychological tests. For older children, testing can also be done by an educator trained in academic assessments to evaluate the child's grade level and the possible presence of a specific learning disability. The purpose of developmental testing is to determine the child's developmental profile. Children with PDD typically do not have a uniform developmental profile; usually they will not be found to have a single developmental age across the spectrum of tested skills. For example, children with Autistic

Disorder often function at age level or above in visual-perception (for example, puzzle skills) and visual-motor skills (eye-hand coordination, for drawing simple geometric shapes, for example); in contrast, they may function significantly below age level in the areas of expressive and receptive language. We also observe that children with PDD often do well on developmental testing but demonstrate significant impairments in adaptive functioning, defined as the application of intelligence to daily living skills such as greeting people and answering the telephone appropriately. Several specific instruments are used to assess adaptive functioning during developmental evaluations.

Speech and Language Assessment

Children with PDD always have some degree of communication impairment, and so speech and language assessments are part of the full evaluation. These assessments include informal observations of the child's use of language in natural play and in conversation, as well as standardized speech and language tests. For PDD children who are able to speak in sentences, the assessment becomes more complex and encompasses all aspects of language, for example, articulation, vocabulary, syntax (sentence structure), sentence length, grammar, and prosody (the tonal quality of speech). This assessment allows evaluation not only of the child's expressive and receptive language but also the ability to use language socially. The social use of language, called pragmatics, includes skills such as greeting others, initiating conversations, sustaining conversations, and reading facial expressions. The purpose of these assessments is to determine the child's communication strengths and weaknesses and to design an individual communication treatment program. It is to the child's distinct advantage that the speech and language assessment be carried out by the same therapist who will eventually be providing the child's speech and language therapy.

Medical Evaluation

The goal of the medical assessment is to determine whether the child has a medical condition that could be causing the PDD symptoms and to determine if there are treatments, such as medications, that could effectively relieve these symptoms. This part of the evaluation can be carried out by professionals from the appropriate medical disciplines, including developmental pediatricians, pediatric neurologists, pediatric geneticists, and child psychiatrists. This evaluation consists of a through physical examination and a behavioral assessment; a neurological examination and specific laboratory studies may also be necessary. Common laboratory studies include DNA testing for Fragile X Syndrome and chromosomal testing for chromosomal abnormalities, such as translocation, which are sometimes associated with PDD. The physician may also order an electroencephalogram and magnetic resonance imaging of the head.

Occupational Therapy Assessment

Many children with PDDs have delays in gross or fine motor skills, or both. Although the developmental testing evaluates all areas of development including motor skills, the assessment is broad and can be considered a screen. Thus, when a child demonstrates delays in motor skills during testing, a referral is usually made to an occupational therapist for a more extensive assessment. It is typical for children with PDD to have adequate gross motor skills but to demonstrate difficulties in more complex motor coordination, like the skill required to kick a ball. In the area of fine motor skills, a child with PDD can have problems using scissors, drawing pictures, forming letters, or manipulating fasteners on clothing. These skills are systematically evaluated by occupational therapists using standardized tests.

TREATMENT

Treating children with PDD is complex and requires a multi-disciplinary approach. Treatment is dependent on many variables, including the specific PDD diagnosis and the child's communication skills, intellectual level, educational abilities, and adaptive functioning. The treatment for a mute autistic child with a low IQ will be very different from the treatment for a child with Asperger's Disorder, whose academic skills are above grade level. Nevertheless, there is a core of treatment concerns and approaches common to most PDDs. The overall goals for treatment are to (1) improve socialization skills, (2) improve communication skills, (3) eliminate behavioral problems, and (4) seek to develop age-appropriate cognitive and adaptive skills.

Parent Education

The child's parents are the most important members of the treatment team. Treatment thus begins by educating the parents about all aspects of their child's disorder. In the clinic we review the *DSM-IV* diagnostic criteria so that the parents understand exactly how the diagnosis was made. We also provide them with a historical perspective. This is particularly helpful for parents of children with PDD-NOS or Asperger's Disorder; by understanding the history of the disorder, parents are better able to understand the relationship between these disorders and autism. Since these diagnoses are confusing, we spend the necessary time to clarify any misconceptions.

We also spend a good deal of time reviewing the results of developmental testing, to help the parents understand at what age level their child is currently functioning in both language and visual skills. We provide information regarding what is known about the neurology of PDD, and we emphasize that scientists are studying the neurological causes of PDD, which currently are not understood. The child's prognosis is discussed, and we attempt to provide the parents with a range of likely possible outcomes for their child, recognizing that these can be only best guesses or approximations. Parents are also provided with list of local parent support groups. The Autism Society of America, for instance, is a well-established group of parents and professionals. It has a national office, and many communities have local chapters. Another and growing resource is the Internet, particularly the newsgroup bit.listserv.autism. In addition, we encourage parents to educate themselves about all aspects of PDD and to this end provide them with a list of reference books covering assessment and treatment of PDD; these include the two books by Bryna Siegel and Michael Powers.

Behavioral Treatment

All children with PDD benefit from behavioral approaches. My experience as a special education teacher helped me to recognize the value of a well-thought-out behavioral program for children with PDD. These programs help children focus their attention on appropriate activities and thus increase their ability to learn. I also found that children who had difficulty tolerating unanticipated change responded positively to an increased measure of routine and structure in their daily schedules. For example, we might provide a twelve-year-old child with Asperger's Disorder with a written daily schedule to carry in his pocket. He can then refer to it and so anticipate changes scheduled for that day. Many times specific behavioral problems such as aggressive behaviors can be managed with a well-designed individualized behavioral program.

Young children with autistic disorder and other PDDs usually perform best with intensive behavioral educational programs. A variety of behavioral philosophies have been applied to the treatment of children with PDD. Common features of these intensive approaches are initial one-to-one instruction that is faded to small group instruction, approximately twenty to thirty hours a week of instruction, and tasks that are developmentally appropriate. For instance a three-year-old child functioning at a twenty-four-month level would be given tasks appropriate to the twenty-four-month level rather than at the child's chronological age level. Not all approaches will be applicable to all PDD children, and so behavioral approaches must be individualized to the needs and learning style of each child. Therapists, teachers, and parents who work with PDD children using these behavioral programs must be trained by an experienced specialist who has had extensive experience in applying these programs to children with PDD. Behavioral programs are most beneficial when applied in the school and at home.

Education

Most children with PDD require specialized education. Typically a child with Autistic Disorder will be placed in a special education classroom. The advantages of special education are a lower teacher-to-student ratio, teachers with specialized training (including training in behavioral-based techniques), and a curriculum individualized to each child's developmental level.

Some children with a PDD, including a few with Autistic Disorder, are mainstreamed into the regular classroom. These children may nevertheless need supplemental services, which can include a one-to-one aide to help them in the regular classroom, speech and language therapy, and social training therapy. Another common practice is the use of a resource specialist. In this approach, the child attends a regular classroom and each day or each week meets with the resource specialist for special education services in specific subjects. As the child's individual education needs change, so do the type and level of special education. The current trend in education is to have the child make the transition to mainstreaming as soon as appropriate. Some individuals continue in special education until the age of twenty-two years, the expected age of graduation for persons with severe learning impairments. Following this they attend a specialized adult work program.

Speech and Language

Speech and language therapy is part of the treatment program for most children with a PDD diagnosis. For children who have limited verbal language, the therapy focuses on verbal imitation in addition to alternative forms of communication. An alternative form of communication typically incorporates pictures of familiar objects and activities on a board so the child can point to a picture to communicate what he or she wants. Pictures can also be used to make a picture schedule so the child has something concrete to refer to throughout the day; in this way, the child can anticipate the events of the day and so reduce frustration and resulting tantrums. For children with more verbal language, therapy focuses on articulation, appropriate sentence structure, communicative use of language, and the social use of language. For higher-functioning children like those with Asperger's Disorder, speech and language therapy stresses the more sophisticated social uses of language, for example, topic maintenance in conversations and appropriate greeting behaviors when greeting peers in contrast to greeting a teacher.

Occupational Therapy

For children who have fine motor and/or gross motor problems, or both, occupational therapy becomes part of their overall treatment plan. Many children with a PDD have significant problems in motor skills and benefit from an individualized occupational treatment program. For example, children with Asperger's Disorder frequently have motor incoordination that interferes with their performance in sports activities and causes their handwriting to be illegible.

Social Training

All of the treatment strategies already mentioned frequently improve the child's social skills, and thus, social training is integrated in almost all aspects of treatment for children with a

PDD. This is because almost any type of learning takes the form of a social event involving student and therapist-teacher interaction. Thus, when a therapist-teacher is working with a PDD child, the initial tasks are to establish eye contact, improve attention to the instructions given by the therapist-teacher, and engage in turn-taking activities. There are also specific therapies directed toward improving peer interactions for children with milder forms of PDD, and these therapies are currently on the increase. Peer-interaction therapies usually consist of small groups of children and one or two therapists. The groups meet weekly after school to learn specific social skills that they then practice together—activities such as sports, board games, cooking, and outings.

Psychopharmacology

Medication for PDD is effective only in the treatment of specific target symptoms; it does not treat the core symptoms of autism such as deficits in socialization and communication. Target symptoms sometimes treated include hyperactivity, short attention span, perseverative behaviors, self-injurious behaviors, and aggressive outbursts. In most cases, behavior modification techniques are more effective than pharmacology, and so medication is indicated only after an adequate trial of behavior modification has failed or sometimes as an adjunct to behavior therapy.

The choice of medication depends on the target symptoms. When treating hyperactivity and poor attention span, I use stimulants such as Ritalin; also, the tricyclic antidepressants used to treat ADHD, such as Tofranil, may be effective. For treating aggressive behaviors and other uncontrollable behavior disturbances, I find that the neuroleptics, especially Haldol and Mellaril, are useful. Recent reports indicate that selective serotonin reuptake inhibitors may be effective in treating the perseverative and ritualized behaviors of children with autism. I have used Prozac, Paxil, and Anafranil to treat aggressive behaviors, perseverative behaviors, and rituals, with variable results.

GATEKEEPERS OF SERVICES

To be an effective advocate for children with PDD, I have found it imperative to be well versed in the various community institutions in the San Francisco Bay Area that are gatekeepers of services. These institutions include managed care organizations, local school districts, and county regional centers (county centers that provide services for children and adults with developmental disorders). My approach to these institutions is to become familiar with them and their various policies regarding the assessment and treatment of PDD.

Many managed care organizations regard autism and the other PDD diagnoses as mutually exclusive diagnoses. I am frequently told by these organizations that they do not serve this population because PDDs are "developmental disorders," which are served by the schools. Some managed care organizations authorize the initial evaluation, but they usually do not authorize critical treatment services such as behavior and language therapy. Medication treatment is frequently authorized if it is done by a pediatrician or neurologist but often not if it is carried out by a psychiatrist because of the restrictions the insurers place on mental health services. Since this is a specialized field and there are only a few PDD clinics in the Bay Area, our clinic is often not on the family's managed care provider list. Thus, for the initial evaluation, parents have to request authorization outside their network or else pay for clinical services out-of-pocket. What I have found helpful in my clinic is to develop a comprehensive description of the evaluation procedure including the billing codes for specific services, thus setting up a package assessment. After I made this adjustment, I found that more managed care companies were willing to cover the initial multidisciplinary evaluation.

It happens that many of the recommendations that I make for a given child are for services that could be available through the school or regional center. To get services through the schools or regional centers, the child must meet eligibility criteria, which are frequently based on the diagnosis. It is common practice throughout the United States that a child with PDD must have a diagnosis of Autistic Disorder to receive certain services. Children with other PDD diagnoses such as PDD-NOS or Asperger's Disorder frequently receive limited services or no services at all from these organizations.

Thus, the diagnosis of Autistic Disorder is a ticket for services through the schools and regional centers, but usually not through managed care organizations. Children with a diagnosis of PDD-NOS or Asperger's Disorder are sometimes excluded from services by all providers, a serious problem for these children and their families. It is unfortunate that providers use categorical *DSM* diagnoses as eligibility criteria for services. This practice seems especially arbitrary when we recognize that these disorders are not well understood and seem to change with each revision of the *DSM*. A more enlightened policy would base eligibility for services on specific symptoms and specific developmental delays (for example, testing results documenting functional language impairments).

PROGNOSIS

Historically, autism has been considered one of the most devastating of the childhood psychiatric disorders. Part of the reason was that prior to about 1985, only the more severe cases of PDD were evaluated, and classical autism was the primary diagnosis given. Individuals with this diagnosis usually remained significantly impaired throughout their lives. They were not able to live independently and so were placed in specialized institutions or remained at home with their parents. Only a minority of them achieved independence as adults. Those few who did achieve independence tended to have the twin hallmarks of speaking in sentences and a normal IQ by the age of six years.

Today when a child is given the diagnosis of autism or one of the related disorders, the diagnosis need not always be associated with such an unhappy outcome. As I have discussed, the diagnostic criteria have altered with time. Milder cases are now diagnosed, at a younger age, and several new diagnostic categories are used. Children as young as eighteen to twenty-four months may now receive a tentative PDD diagnosis. We have come to recognize milder forms of autism: high-functioning autism, PDD-NOS, and Asperger's Disorder. Only during the past decade or so have patients been diagnosed at a very young age or diagnosed with relatively mild symptoms; for this reason, long-term clinical follow-up has not been possible, and so the prognosis of such cases remains uncertain. It is my impression that many of these children will have a generally favorable outcome, including full integration into society. Thus, it seems likely that the prognosis for these younger and/or milder cases of PDD, which formerly might have gone undiagnosed, is relatively good, but only time will tell. In addition, benefits stemming from earlier and more effective behavioral interventions have been impressive. These developments in diagnosis and treatment hold out increased hope for PDD children and their families.

What excites me about my work with these families is that I can help parents understand their child's PDD in the context of constantly changing diagnosis, treatment, and neurobiological research. Often parents are confused by these diagnoses because they assume diagnostic and therapeutic categories are fixed and unchangeable. By helping parents understand PDD in this rapidly changing milieu, I can help them become better advocates for their children.

NOTES

P. 28, *Dr. Leo Kanner, an American psychiatrist:* Kanner, L. (1943). Autistic disturbances of affective contact. *The Nervous Child, 2,* 217–250.

P. 30, *The twelve DSM-IV diagnostic criteria for autism:* American Psychiatric

Association. (1994). *Diagnostic and statistical manual of mental disorders* (4th ed.). Washington, DC: Author.

P. 33, *the PDD-NOS child exhibits fewer than six of the twelve DSM-IV diagnostic criteria for autism:* American Psychiatric Association. (1994).*Diagnostic and statistical manual of mental disorders* (4th ed.). Washington, DC: American Psychiatric Association.

P. 36, *Dr. Hans Asperger, a Viennese physician:* Asperger H. (1944). Die 'autistischen Psychopathen' im Kindesalter. *Archiv fur Psychiatrie und Nervenkrankheiten, 117,* 76–136.

P. 36, *when Dr. Lorna Wing, an autism researcher in England, used the term Asperger's Syndrome:* Frith, U. (1991). *Autism and Asperger syndrome.* Cambridge: Cambridge University Press.

P. 36, *As defined in the DSM-IV Asperger's Disorder is:* American Psychiatric Association. (1994). *Diagnostic and statistical manual of mental disorders* (4th ed.). Washington, DC: Author.

P. 37, *Rett's Disorder:* Braddock, S. R., Braddock, B. A., & Graham, J. M., Jr. (1993). Rett syndrome: An update and review for the primary pediatrician. *Clinical Pediatrics, 32*(10), 613–626.

P. 38, *Children with Childhood Disintegrative Disorder:* Volkmar, F. R., & Rutter, M. (1995). Childhood disintegrative disorder: Results of the DSM-IV autism field trial. *Journal of the American Academy of Child and Adolescent Psychiatry, 34*(8), 1092–1095.

P. 39, *associated with Asperger's Disorder is nonverbal learning disability:* Rourke, B. P. (Ed.). (1995). *Syndrome of nonverbal learning disabilities: Neurodevelopmental manifestations.* New York: Guilford Press.

P. 43, *A number of well-characterized neurological disorders have been associated with a minority of cases of PDD:* Lotspeich, L. J., & Ciaranello, R. D. (1993). The neurobiology and genetics of infantile autism. In R. Bradley & R. Harris (Eds.), *International review of neurobiology.* San Diego: Academic Press.

P. 50, *Treating children with PDD is complex:* Quill, K. A. (1995). *Teaching children with autism.* Albany, NY: Delmar.

P. 51, *The Autism Society of America:* 7910 Woodmont Ave., Suite 650, Bethesda, MD 20814. Phone: 1–800–3AU-TISM; or Web site: http://www.autism-society.org.

P. 51, *these include the two books by Bryna Siegel and Michael Powers:* Siegel, B. (1996). *The world of the autistic child: Understanding and treatment of autistic spectrum disorders.* New York: Oxford University Press; Powers, M. D. (1989). *Children with autism: A parents' guide.* Rockville, MD: Woodbine House.

P. 51, *intensive behavioral educational programs:* Dawson, G., & Osterling, J. (1996). Early intervention in autism. In M. J. Guralnick (Ed.), *The effectiveness of early intervention.* Baltimore: Paul Brookes Publishing Co.

P. 54, *There are also specific therapies . . . for children with milder forms of PDD:* Quill, K. A. (1995). *Teaching children with autism.* Albany, NY: Delmar.

P. 54, *Medication for PDD:* Cook, E. H., & Leventhal, B. (1995). Autistic disorder and other pervasive developmental disorders. *Child and Adolescent Psychiatric Clinics of North America: Pediatric Pharmacology II,* 4(2).

3

SLEEP DISTURBANCES

Maria Villalba Devera

Questions related to sleep frequently arise in primary care offices during routine child visits. Parents may approach the topic with concern and wonder if their child's sleeping pattern is normal for this age. These questions are often motivated by the fact that the child resists bedtime and the parents are eager to have their own sleeping patterns return to normal. Parents do not usually seek psychiatric evaluation unless their own attempts at alleviating the problem have failed, or when their pediatrician suspects there may be a psychopathologic process evolving or evident. The most common referral to a mental health professional for the preschool-age child is related to complaints of dysregulation of sleep. A primary insomnia diagnosis is rare in this age group; the more common case typically involves protodyssomnia, or the inability to fall asleep and the occurrence of frequent nighttime awakening.

Difficulty falling asleep, as well as frequent awakening, occurs in 15 to 20 percent of the normal toddler and preschool population. An assessment of this common situation begins with a careful history of the child, with particular attention to external factors such as the parents' routines, household daily patterns, the family's culture, other people in the home, noise levels, the child's sleep place, the environment, and parent-child attachment. Internal factors as well should be considered, such as the child's temperament, resilience, individual response to reactions to stimuli such as hunger, pain, hot and cold temperatures, and ability to self-soothe when parents or caregivers are not available. The child's history will provide you with a snapshot of a typical day, as in the case of Todd.

TODD

Todd is the eighteen-month-old firstborn son of two professional parents who work full time. Since his birth, Todd's mother and father have been engaged parents, reading "about every book out there" and following up religiously with the pediatrician's advice on how to get Todd to sleep. Their practice was to put Todd down in his room, shut the door, and let him scream until he fell asleep. Eventually one of them would give in and go to him to offer comfort.

I learned from Todd's parents that he wakes up at 6:00 A.M. Monday through Friday. His parents describe their mornings as hurried and scrambled and say that Todd can be cranky and whiny, but for the most part, he eventually wakes up and is dropped off by 7:00 at day care without a major fuss.

At day care, Todd naps about one hour in the late morning from 11:00 until lunchtime, and then later in the afternoon from about 3:00 until 5:00. His parents take turns picking him up at 6:00, and eventually everyone arrives home at 6:30. No one else lives in the home, and Todd's parents describe themselves as having a stable relationship, happy marriage, and mutual job satisfaction. They said that Todd's birth was planned and greatly anticipated, and that they share in caregiving responsibilities.

When they arrive home, one of them makes attempts to play with Todd, while the other prepares dinner, returns phone calls, and watches the news on television. Todd is usually "full of energy" until the late evening. Dinner activities usually wind down by 8:30, but his parents admit to pushing dinner and evening activities back an additional hour occasionally.

Todd's parents said that they did not believe in having a strict bedtime, and they sometimes allowed Todd to stay up, especially on the weekends, figuring that it is important to take advantage of their whole day together and that he could sleep later the following morning. They view themselves as consistent parents, with bedtime rituals and routines of clothes changing, teeth brushing, singing, listening to music, or reading before bed. What has taken the greatest toll on them, however, has been the increasingly prolonged bedtime ritual.

When I asked them how other caregivers, such as grandparents or babysitters, have done with Todd, they acknowledged that it can also take the others just as long, but that the others do not appear to have the battle that ensues when they attempt turning off the light.

Todd's parents report that his temperament is consistent with being an "easy" child (as opposed to "slow to warm up" or "difficult") as defined by Thomas and Chess. He is described as a "good child" in day care as well as by other caregivers. His parents also report that Todd does well under stressful stimuli, such as hunger, hot and cold, or pain. They proudly state that Todd has not needed to have stuffed animals or a blanket, and he does not suck his thumb. These objects, though described as "transitional objects" in children by Winnicott, are also know as "self-soothing" aids to help provide comfort to the child in the absence of parents.

SLEEP STAGES AND PATTERNS

Before addressing how Todd's parents might begin to change his sleeping behavior, we must understand more about a toddler's sleeping stages and patterns.

Sleep physiology is a fairly new concept. It emerged with Aserinsky and Kleitman in 1953, who described the REM (rapid eye movement or active sleep) and NREM (non–rapid eye movement or passive sleep) of ultradian organization.

Toddlers' sleep patterns are based on the function of basic sleep-wake architecture or organization. These internal factors (circadian rhythms composed of diurnal and nocturnal rhythms and ultradian rhythms) are closely interrelated with the external and internal factors mentioned previously.

Circadian Rhythms

Circadian rhythm is a biological clock that is present in every living organism. In humans, the circadian rhythm corresponds to a twenty-five-hour period of time that organizes diurnal (day) and nocturnal (night) cycles for wake and sleep patterns, as well as synchronizing other physiological functions (for example, body temperature, urine excretion, and cortisol excretion) during this period of time. Circadian rhythm wake and sleep patterns establish themselves at four months of age, and a nocturnal sleep pattern continues to solidify progressively until the child reaches six to seven months of age. Time periods of ages six to seven months, ten to twelve months, and thirteen to fifteen months are also found to correlate with ultradian rhythms and continue throughout the child's development.

Ultradian Rhythms

Ultradian rhythms are shorter biological cycles (defined as less than a day). Ultradian organization related to sleep refers to alternating cycles of REM (active) sleep and NREM (passive) sleep lasting initially from fifty to sixty minutes in infants and toddlers and eventually reaching a ninety-minute period in adolescence and adulthood.

Just as there are shifts in time periods with cycle length, there are also shifts in the amount of REM and NREM that occurs as an infant and toddler develops. Developmentally, the ultradian sleep cycle of children one to five years of age is characterized by a sleep latency period (period of falling asleep) of fifteen to thirty minutes, which influences the stability of cycle rhythm. In infants, initially, there is 50 percent of REM sleep. Later, at one year of age, the amount of REM sleep decreases to 30 to 35 percent, and at two to five years of age it decreases further to 20 to 25 percent of the total sleep time, which is the average amount seen in adulthood. As REM sleep decreases, so does the infant's normal motoric movements, such as facial twitches and grimaces. Another developmental change seen at this time is that NREM progressively begins replacing REM sleep in the early period of the cycle, and NREM sleep differentiates into four separate stages by four months of age. These four separate stages correspond to distinct brain wave patterns that are seen by EEG (electroencephalogram) instrumentation.

Stage 1 (NREM) corresponds to low-frequency waves on EEG and is the transitional state between wake and sleep. This also corresponds to changes in muscle tone that are measured by EMG (electomyogram). In this stage there is a small decrease in muscle tone from wakefulness. Eye movement is slow, rolling, and involuntary.

In *Stage 2 (NREM)*, the brain waves change to theta waves (4–7 Hz) with superimposed bursts of higher-frequency waves called sleep spindles and K complexes that are 0.5 to 1.5 seconds in duration and are in the range of 14 to 16 Hz. Muscle tone is further reduced, and there is a corresponding reduction in eye activity.

In *Stages 3 and 4 (NREM)*, the waves change to high amplitude and low frequency (0.5–3.0) and are now called delta waves. These two stages differ only in the amount of waves in each phase: Stage 3 with delta waves at 20 to 50 percent and Stage 4 with delta waves at 50 percent. During these stages, muscle tone further decreases and is low, and eye movements are rarely seen.

REM, or active sleep, is characterized by higher brain wave activity and is usually the time when dreams occur. During this period of sleep, muscle tone is actually suppressed. Eye movement is typically rapid, conjugate, and sharp. Also, changes in the autonomic system are seen by fluctuations in sympathetic and parasympathetic regulation with effects on cardiac function and muscle tone. In toddlers, as the ultradian rhythm undergoes progressive development, their sleep requirements also change in a decreasing fashion, from thirteen hours for the two year old, to eleven and a half hours for the four year old, and nine and a half hours for the six year old.

Measuring Sleep Activity

Instrumentation has made defining sleep activity possible. The standard in measuring is polysomongraphy, which includes EEG, EMG, electro-oculogram (EOG), and cardiorespiratory monitoring. These means of measurement require electrode placement and collaboration from a toddler, which may not always be easy.

The unfamiliar surroundings of a laboratory or hospital evoke changes in a toddler's normal state, which makes accurate recording difficult. Normal and standardized studies in infants and toddlers are few. Most information about sleep is obtained from measuring daytime naps or one night of sleep. The development of home instrumentation, time-lapse video recording, mattress sensors, direct behavior observation, and most recently actigraphic sensors (wristwatch-like detectors) have been used. These means have been used by themselves or together in attempts to clarify sleep patterns and parent-child interactions around patterns of sleep and wake.

Direct observation is a method frequently used in young children, in a controlled setting or at home. Parents are asked to keep a journal or log as a first step in identifying interactions and bedtime events.

∽

Sleep patterns are made up of a complexity of intertwined stages and cycles. It is easy to see how inconsistencies in Todd's schedule evolved into sleep difficulties. Todd's well-meaning parents unknowingly influenced, and even reinforced, his troubling sleep behavior.

It is important to ask parents to be honest in their desire to influence change in their child's behavior, since, as in Todd's case, succeeding in changing Todd's behavior meant changing their own behavior as well. In my work, I have found that parents who are truly committed to wanting to change are usually more open to parent education and understanding the importance of consistency on a daily basis.

After assessing Todd's routines from the daily journal his parents kept, we were able to see that Todd's afternoon nap, being so late in the day, was causing him to feel rested and not ready to go to bed in the evening. I recommended that his parents consider moving up his afternoon nap to an earlier time, to space out the time between his nap and bedtime.

After fully acknowledging their feelings of guilt around work and sharing time with Todd, his parents were able to gain insight into their own part in Todd's behavior, and they were able to adapt a better perspective of the situation. Although they recognized that their evening times together were limited, they also recognized the benefit of setting a consistent bedtime for Todd at 8:00 P.M. They were able to see that their desire to "do it all" during their limited evening time together worked against decreasing Todd's stimulation prior to bedtime, and they agreed to see that bedtime rituals (changing, teeth brushing, and washing) were done in a more timely manner and with a better awareness of potential stalling tactics on Todd's part. By adhering to a preset amount of before-sleep reading time and planning strategies that would help them troubleshoot difficulties that might arise, they were able to influence how quickly Todd went to bed and lessen the chances of his awakening during the night.

TREATMENT

Defining sleep problems in toddlers varies from investigator to investigator due to different criteria that are used. Normative data do indicate that 20 to 40 percent of toddlers have difficulties falling asleep and waking up during the night. In general, parents tend to underreport difficulties of falling asleep and awaking at night. Crowell and colleagues in 1987, in a study of one hundred middle-class toddlers between eighteen and thirty-six months of age, found that 25 percent of these children had a latency in sleep onset greater than thirty minutes.

Because of wide variables in normative data and insufficient data, separating out toddlers with a clearly defined disorder is difficult. Some data suggest that approximately 25 percent of toddlers suffer from sleep disturbances. It has been suggested that this group of children who are poor sleepers have other influencing factors. For example, infants may have poor central nervous system development–related perinatal problems, or medical problems such as allergies, respiratory, cardiac, or other chronic illnesses. Toddlers described as having temperament difficulties may also be poor sleepers and have problems being able to self-soothe. Benoit and colleagues, in 1992, reviewed previous literature on the possible influence that attachment to primary caretakers and anxiety related to separation might play in sleep difficulties. Ainsworth's theory of attachment suggests that children who are insecurely attached may have more anxiety and therefore increased difficulty separating from their caregiver. This may manifest itself in sleep refusal and escalating oppositional behavior at bedtime.

Pharmacotherapy

By glancing at Table 3.1, it appears that plentiful treatment options are available for toddlers. Often parents want a quick solution and ask about safe medications. Unfortunately, there is little information on pharmacotherapy in toddlers, and what is known applies to only the limited number of medications that have been looked at. Russo and colleagues in 1976 looked at diphenhydramine for sleep onset and nighttime awakening. Richman in 1985 noted less nighttime awakening in children treated with niaprazine. Of these medications, diphenhydramine is most often used. These medications that have been tried in the toddler age group have shown short-term benefits, but long-term efficacy has not been seen. Established safety of medications in toddlers, optimal dosing, and potential side effects, including possibilities of rebound once medication is discontinued, were investigated by Weitzman in 1981. Other medications,

Table 3.1
Treatment Options for Toddlers

Explorative	*Behavioral*	*Education*	*Chronotherapy*	*Pharmacotherapy (The Last Resort)*
Psycho-therapy	Extinction delay	Parents	Phase	Diphenhydramine
Dyadic therapy	Gradual extinction	Other caregivers	Phase advance	
	Cueing			
	Shaping			
	Scheduled awakening			
	Positive reinforcement			

which are used in the adult population, such as benzodiazepines and over-the-counter preparations containing alcohol, should not be administered to children for sleep problems.

Behavioral Approaches

A wide variety of behavioral techniques have been shown to be effective with toddlers; however, parental compliance is often the pitfall with these methods. These approaches are more successful when used in combination with other treatment approaches, as listed in Table 3.1. Parental support with reassurance and education can be the key. Parents often find it stressful to ignore their child's crying during some approaches that ask them to withhold response. Cognitive reconstructive strategies have helped parents learn new ways to cope during these times.

The following techniques may be used, alone or in combination.

Extinction. This is defined as a process where a particular behavior diminishes because it is no longer reinforced when it occurs. In protodyssomnias in toddlers, parents or other caregivers withhold their attention to their child's angry protest at bedtime or nighttime awakening. If a toddler wanders into the parents' room, the parents' interactions with the child are minimized. The parents keep their interaction brief, make minimal eye contact, and with little response redirect their child gently but firmly back to bed.

Gradual Extinction. Gradual extinction is the progressive diminishment of a particular behavior through a lack of reinforcement. Forms of gradual extinction are at times preferred by parents, because they do not have to deal with lengthy protests of crying during nighttime awakening. In treating for sleep problems, gradual extinction can be combined with scheduled awakening: the parents awaken the child twenty to thirty minutes before the child usually wakes up in the middle of the night and comfort the child as if he or she had awakened on his or her own. Gradually behavioral changes are seen as this technique decreases the spontaneous awakening habit and extinguishes previous unwanted behavior.

Shaping. This technique is also defined as operant conditioning that is used in behavior therapy. A behavior goal is set and then reached step by step, with specific reinforcers along the way as the child gets closer to the desired sleep behavior.

Positive Reinforcement. In this widely used technique, the consequences of a desired behavior are rewarded to increase the probability that it will occur again. It is successful and used often for bedtime settling problems in older toddlers. For example, a toddler's parents first establish the desired time of bedtime, say, 8:00 P.M. Targets for positive reinforcements include the child's going to bed, staying in bed, not screaming, and returning to bed if necessary with little or no protest. Reinforcers for desired behavior are generally awarded in the morning. For example, a sticker or star may be given for each desired behavior and then placed on a chart that is easily visible and centrally located in the home. Positive reinforcement alone or in combination with this and other techniques has also been effective. Richman in 1985 found a 77 percent significant effectiveness of marked or completed improvement in 4.4 sessions in children one to five years of age in combined treatment.

Education

Education allows parents and caregivers greater understanding and helps them feel supported in their efforts. Parents often feel anxious and guilty if they sense they are not providing appropriately for their child. For example, parents typically feel that they need to respond to a child who cries at night. With awareness, parents may learn to understand their contribution to the nightly wailing. Once a toddler has the proper rest, parents can have theirs, which in turn improves child-parent interactions.

Chronotherapy

Chronotherapy is based on chronobiology or biological rhythms. The human body has multiple rhythms varying in length and function that can be measured. Biological rhythms, seen in body temperature, hormonal levels, and sleep-wake cycles, are set by internal and external synchronizers called "zeitebers" or "time givers." All rhythms have a natural relationship to one another, and when there is a healthy state, rhythms are said to be *in phase*. Changes in sleep patterns like delayed sleep throw off other rhythms, such as cortisol and growth hormone, and are considered to be *out of phase*. Dysregulation of rhythm is called *phase advance* when beginning earlier than usual and *phase delay* when beginning later than usual.

Using these rhythms to reset the clock has been found useful. Light exposure using sunlight or artificial light in combination with time adjustments helps shift sleep cycles. In toddlers, we advance the sleep phase in increments slowly by fifteen minutes every night if the goal is to have the child wake up later. Delaying sleep phase is used to reset the clock that runs closer to twenty-five hours than twenty-four hours. Initially, we let the toddler fall asleep at the time the child normally wants to fall asleep; then we gradually push the schedule back fifteen minutes every night until reaching one to two hours after the previously set bedtime. In the morning, bright light also serves as a cue in setting awakening time, a strong factor in circadian rhythms.

Explorative

Reassessment and evaluation of the child's and caregiver's interactions should be considered a standard approach. Behavior techniques are not always easy to implement, but they can be successful if implemented appropriately. If a caregiver is having relationship problems with a partner or the child, or both, he or she may not be consistent and may provide only intermittent reinforcement, which may reinforce negative behavior. Dyadic therapy, of both child and caregiver, may be helpful to understanding their interactions and may allow you to identify anything that may be impeding a healthy relationship. Play therapy with an emphasis on psychotherapeutic dynamics may also give avenues of understanding in puzzling cases, as often seen in children who have experienced trauma.

CO-SLEEPING

Co-sleeping is another factor that has importance in directly affecting a child's and parents' sleep patterns. Definitions of co-sleeping vary. It has been defined as a child's sleeping in his parents' or caregivers' company in the child's bedroom or the parents' bedroom, or a sleeping room where everyone sleeps. The amount of shared sleeping time could be minutes, hours, part of the night, or all night. Definitions of frequency also vary, from as often as nightly to a few times a week, to once a month or once every 6 months. Some may include in the definition the occasional time when a child is ill or for economic reasons, like sharing rooms while on vacation. Other co-sleeping variables include physical arrangements, which can vary from sleeping in the same room in different beds, to sharing the same bed space. Despite the variables in definitions, questions often come up around this controversial topic.

Sears (1985) supported the idea of the family bed. Positive effects described in five and six year olds were secure feelings, strong self-esteem, and greater autonomy. It is felt that this is achieved when the child seeks private space and wants to move to a bed of his or her own. Those opposed to co-sleeping argue that this practice can eventually lead to sexualized types of behavior. Risk of sexual abuse has been suggested, but there is no evidence to support this. However, this is of clinical concern when assessing co-sleeping. It is important to take a careful account of each situation, balancing an objective perspective with cultural considerations.

Cultural variables make the topic of co-sleeping particularly complex and important. In the United States, primary care providers often frown on co-sleeping, and many reputable pediatrics associations and groups support separate sleeping quarters for children and adults, which they perceive as the norm. Separate sleeping quarters are actually a fairly new idea that began as part of the American norm at the beginning of the century. Co-sleeping prior to this time was acceptable, and it is the norm in most cultures throughout the world.

It is important for you to look at the overall picture, bring the family and child's cultural perspective into your assessment, and keep in mind your own cultural biases and practices. Despite pediatric advice to the contrary, as many as 50 percent of parents eventually co-sleep, with rates varying from 12 percent to 70 percent. A breakdown by culture shows that about 70 percent of African-American toddlers co-sleep, compared with 45 to 50 percent of Hispanic-Americans (with no specific breakdown of area of ethnicity). Co-sleeping is found more in multiple families sharing the same home and with biological parents versus stepparents. It is clear that overcrowded housing may contribute to co-sleeping, but there is unclear information that lower social economic status is a factor.

The most consistent information that has been found with co-sleeping is that it decreases in frequency with age.

Co-sleeping overall is underreported in the United States, and therefore difficult to assess, because it is considered outside the norm. The normative American culture sees co-sleeping as negatively influencing the child's autonomy and views it as a signal of relationship problems with the environment and the parents' inability to set limits with a toddler. Co-sleeping can be seen as an attempt by parents to problem-solve in a situation for which they are unable to provide adequate solutions—for example, after a child has experienced a trauma or as an attempt to defuse a problem relationship by serving as a way to stabilize a dysfunctional marriage. In other cultures, such as Pacific Islander, Asian, Samoan, African-American, and Hispanic, co-sleeping is viewed more positively and is more readily accepted. Caudill (1969) and Plath (1973) viewed Japanese facilities and reported the co-sleeping served as "nurturant family bonds rather than lack of space of sexual impulses." In Chinese families, co-sleeping is common, and it supports how families function as a unit rather than individually. In African-American culture, independence is valued, but so are interdependence and relatedness to others.

Cultural variables may also be seen in attitudes toward self-soothing techniques. In the United States, self-soothing techniques and the use of transitional objects are commonly accepted and considered healthy and a normal part of development. In other cultures, these objects or thumb sucking may be viewed negatively and are not supported. As you evaluate a child for sleep disturbances, it is important to take into account the external factors associated with co-sleeping (such as being awakened by someone else's movements) and the internal factors (such as the child's development of self-soothing abilities). Further studies are needed to look at the relationship between toddlers' co-sleeping behaviors and their association with self-soothing. It empirically appears that co-sleepers have less need for self-soothing objects. Also we need additional studies examining the difference between children who begin co-sleeping with their parents early in infancy, as compared to reactive co-sleeping, which occurs in the second year of life after the infant has slept alone.

NIGHTMARES AND NIGHT TERRORS

Three-and-a-half-year-old Kelly was described by her parents as a good sleeper until recently, when she began crying in the middle of the night and waking them up because of bad dreams. She would usually wake up and recount the whole story to her parents and then be afraid to go back to sleep. She says she sees monsters and ugly things on the ceiling.

Nightmares, or parasomnias, are common in toddlers three to five years of age. They are thought to be related to the ongoing development of a child's imagination and fantasy during this stage, and most toddlers can recall their nightmares the following morning.

Nightmares typically occur during REM sleep, during the latter third of the night, and usually in the early morning hours. They are thought to be related to an active imagination, familial predisposition, and psychological stress (insecurity, separation, toilet training, or traumatic events). Nightmares are also seen in children with febrile illness and, more often, in children who have central nervous system disease, mental retardation, or depression as well as in children who take medications that increase REM sleep (for example, tricyclic antidepressants, reserpine, beta-blockers, levodopa, cholinesterase inhibitors, monoamine oxidase inhibitors, and digoxin). Children who discontinue a REM-suppressant medication, such as barbiturates, benzodiazepines, and amphetamines, may experience rebound nightmares.

Children usually outgrow nightmares and require minimal intervention. In general, it is helpful to reduce stressful factors that may contribute to the problem and to encourage the child to verbalize his or her fears. If nightmares continue at a rate of about two per week over a period of six months, further psychological assessment may be indicated with possibilities of more aggressive treatment.

Unlike nightmares, sleep terrors, or pavor nocturnus, are a partial arousal state of sleep that occurs in the first third of the night, in the NREM Stage 4 sleep. Usually children have no memory of the event and return to sleep quickly. There is no interaction during the event except for agitations that at times require someone to help prevent a child from injury if he or she, for example, runs toward a window or the street. Predisposing factors may be genetic, developmental, sleep deprivation, an inconsistent sleep-wake schedule, or psychological factors. Preregulatory (or predisposing) factors of the endogenous type are obstructive sleep apnea, gastroesophageal reflux, surgery, fever, and occasional movement in sleep. Examples of exogenous type factors are stimulate tactile, auditory sense, and drugs used.

Jeremy, four and a half years old, came to our clinic for treatment with night terrors.

JEREMY

Jeremy lives with his parents and older sister in an affluent area of town. His parents described a previous day as being full of fun. Jeremy had played with friends at a birthday party, followed by playing outside with friends and watching an exciting and funny video. The evening had been uneventful otherwise, and the usual bedtime routine had been carried out.

His parents said that shortly after everyone had been in bed, they heard Jeremy let out a shriek. When they ran to see what was going on, Jeremy, agitated, sweating, crying, and screaming, was running out of his room. His eyes appeared wide and open, but he was unresponsive to their attempts to speak to or comfort him. They described him as becoming increasingly "wild." Eventually, Jeremy's agitation dissipated, and he returned to sleep.

The next morning, Jeremy's parents questioned him about the previous night. He had no recollection of what had happened.

Parents are often frightened by this unusual and strange experience, and it is important to reassure them that night terrors are usually self-limiting and benign. They should be instructed to think about safety and to keep the child in an area where he or she will be prevented from running out into the street or jumping onto objects that could be potentially harmful. Mental imagery and relaxation have been found to be useful with children who have more frequent episodes. Medications such as benzodiazepines and tricyclics have also been used short term in more difficult cases. But most often, no intervention is needed, and only safety guarding is recommended.

In more resistant cases with frequent recurrent episodic nocturnal wandering, you should keep in mind the possibility of nocturnal seizures. In these cases, the child may experience daytime sleepiness. Another consideration may be nocturnal paroxysmal dystonia, which is characterized as structural, recurrent, limp movements that occur multiple times nightly. It is believed that this is another form of seizure activity coming from the frontal lobe of the brain. These are considered secondary disorders of arousal, and treatment is similar to diurnal seizures, which are treated with anticonvulsive medications.

SLEEP APNEA

Obstructive sleep apnea is defined as a stop in the airflow taken in via the nose or mouth for ten seconds at least thirty times during a seven-hour sleep period. It is characterized by loud, chronic snoring with mouth breathing, cranky and angry moods in the mornings, difficulties with attention and concentration, and hyperactivity. It is also common to have sleepwalking and enuresis associated with this condition, and it is common in children between the ages of four and six. Because of the obstruction during sleep, this disorder is often accompanied by hypoxemia (lack of oxygen) and hypercapnia (too much carbon dioxide). Further assessment may reveal that apneic episodes, which are associated with lack of oxygen, usually end with the child's gasping or moaning.

JOEY

Joey is a five-year-old who was brought to his pediatrician because of concerns about Attention-Deficit/Hyperactivity Disorder. His preschool and kindergarten teachers complained about his inability to stay seated and to pay attention to stories read in class, as well as his difficulties staying focused on any task. He has been described as running around yet appearing sleepy and fatigued. His parents say that he gets a good night's sleep, but they complain that he chronically snores loudly, causing his older brother to sleep in another room.

Joey's pediatrician administered the Connor Scales test to rule out Attention-Deficit/Hyperactivity Disorder. The scores did show significance for aggression, inattention, and hyperactivity. On physical examination, his pediatrician found Joey to be in good health but did note that his tonsils and adenoids were significantly large and that they had been on previous well visits.

Diagnosis is usually made by means of medical history and physical exam. Sleep polysomnography is used in cases where there is a difficulty establishing the diagnosis. Treatment is adenoidectomy and tonsillectomy, which usually improve symptoms days to weeks postoperatively after swelling goes down and healing takes place. Continuous positive airway pressure (CPAP) is an alternative form of treatment, but it is used only in the short term. CPAP is poorly tolerated by children and may be used while parents contemplate surgery.

Another type of sleep apneic syndrome that is thought to be possibly related is seen in younger infants, between three and nine months old. These infants may have a dysfunction in their involuntary respiratory control mechanisms, which may be related to sudden infant death syndrome (SIDS). It is believed that this might be due to a lack of maturity of the central arousal mechanism, but there is no clear evidence connecting SIDS to sleep apnea. Children with sleep apnea problems have also been found to be mildly growth retarded due to disruptions of Stage 4 NREM sleep, when growth hormones are secreted. Apneic spells are seen throughout the night sleep cycle and have not been determined to be constant in any cycle. More breathing irregularities have been seen with prenatal infants than normal-term neonates.

OTHER SLEEP DISORDERS

There are other sleep disorders found in the psychiatric and neuropsychiatric populations. The sleep disorders found in the psychiatric population are depicted in Table 3.2. Sleep disturbances are seen in mentally retarded children, children with autism, and children with other developmental delays. Also, children with central neurological disorders—as well as children with Tourette's disease, migraine headaches, and Kleine-Levin Syndrome—display sleep disturbances, but these disorders are usually seen in later childhood.

Current limitations in accessing toddlers, such as parents' reluctance, children's developmentally normal and appropriate response to strangers, touch, unfriendly appearing equipment, and laboratory settings, all add to the complexity of attempting to standardize conditions in order to obtain consistent data and normative information. While we have been able to collect data by parental reports, observations, psychological testing,

Table 3.2
Sleep Disturbances in Psychiatric Disorders

Posttraumatic Stress Disorder	*Anxiety*	*Depression*
Nightmares	Difficulty falling asleep	Increased latency and early morning awakening
Frequent awakening	Frequent awakening	Circadian dysregulation
Difficulty falling asleep		
Circadian dysregulation		

videotaping, and actigraphic and polygraphic recording, there has been no established baseline for comparison or in combination of use of these methods' reliability. One area that has been consistent is the variability at looking at sleep difficulties in data collection, definitions, and what constitute a disorder in this age group.

Influencing factors that are important and need further investigation in relation to assessment and treatment are looking at families and their culture, in both the United States and abroad. Examining cross-cultural patterns may be helpful in defining normative data.

NOTES

P. 63, *as defined by Thomas and Chess:* Thomas, A., & Chess, S. (1977). *Temperament and development.* New York: Brunner/Mazel.

P. 63, *though described as "transitional objects" in children by Winnicott:* Winnicott, D. W. (1970). *Therapeutic consultations in child psychiatry.* New York: Basic Books; Winnicott, D. W. (1971). *Therapeutic consultations in child psychiatry.* New York: Basic Books.

P. 63, *It emerged with Aserinsky and Kleitman in 1953:* Aserinsky, E., & Kleitman, N. (1955). A motility cycle in sleeping infants as manifested by ocular and gross bodily activity. *Journal of Applied Physiology, 8,* 11–13.

P. 67, *Crowell and colleagues in 1987:* As quoted in Hopkins, J., Isaacs, C., & Pitterle, P. (1995). A developmental approach to sleep problems in toddlers.

In C. E. Schaefer (Ed.), *Clinical handbook of sleep disorders in children.* Northvale, NJ: Aronson.

P. 68, *Benoit and colleagues, in 1992:* Benoit, D., Jenal, C. H., Boucher, C., & Meinde, K. K. (1992). Sleep disorders in early childhood: Associated with insecure maternal attachment. *Journal of the American Academy of Child and Adolescent Psychiatry, 31*(1).

P. 68, *Ainsworth's theory of attachment suggests:* Ainsworth, M. D. S., & Eichberg, C. (1992). Effects on infant-mother attachment of mother's unresolved loss of an attachment figure or other traumatic experience. In P. Morris, J. Stevenson-Hinde, & C. Parkes (Eds.), *Attachment across the life cycle* (pp. 160–183). New York: Routledge; Ainsworth, M. D. S., Blehar, M., Waters, E., & Wall, S. (1978). *Patterns of attachment: A psychological study of the strange situation.* Hillsdale, NJ: Erlbaum.

P. 68, *Russo and colleagues in 1976:* Russo, R., et al. (1976). The effectiveness of diphenhydramine HCL in pediatric sleep disorders. *Journal of Clinical Pharmacology, 16*(5–6), 284–288.

P. 68, *Richman in 1985:* Richman, N. (1985). A double-blind drug trial of treatment in young children with waking problems. *Journal of Child Psychology and Psychiatry, 26,* 591–598.

P. 69, *Weitzman in 1981:* Weitzman, E. D. (1981). Sleep and its disorder. *Annual Review of Neuroscience, 4,* 381–417.

P. 71, *Richman in 1985:* Richman, N. (1985). *ibid.*

P. 73, *Sears (1985) supported:* Sears, R. (1976). *Patterns of child rearing.* Stanford, CA: Stanford University Press.

P. 74, *Caudill (1969) and Plath (1973):* Caudill, W. (1969). Paper presented at the Conference on Mental Health Research in Asia and the Pacific; Plath, D. W. (1973). Japanese psychology through Japanese literature: Cares of career and careers of caretaking. *Journal of Nervous and Mental Disease, 157*(5), 346–357.

FOR FURTHER READING

Adair, R. H., & Bauchhner, H. (1993). Sleep problems in childhood. *Current Problems in Pediatrics, 96*(1), 147–170.

Alexander, K. C., Leung, M., & Robinson, W. L. M. (n.d.). Nightmares. *Journal of the National Medical Association, 85*(3), 234.

Ali, N. J., Pitson, D. J., & Stradling J. R. (1993). *Archives in Disease in Childhood, 68,* 360–366.

Anders, T. F., & Eileen, L. A. (1997). Pediatric sleep disorders: Review of the past 10 years. *Journal of the American Academy of Child and Adolescent Psychiatry, 36*(1), pp. 12, 13, 18.

Anders, T. F., Sadeh, A., & Appareddy, V. (1995). Normal sleep in neonates and children. In R. Ferber & M. Kryger (Eds.), *Principal and practice of sleep medicine in the child* (pp. 8–13). Philadelphia: Saunders.

Benoit, D., Jenal, C. H., Boucher, C., & Meinde, K. K. (1992). Sleep disorders in early childhood: Associated with insecure maternal attachment. *Journal of the American Academy of Child and Adolescent Psychiatry, 31*(1), 87.

de Roquefeuil, G., Djakovic, M., & Montagner, H. (1993). New data on ontogeny of the child's sleep wake rhythm. *Chronobiology International, 10*(43–53), 14.

Guilleminault, C. (Ed.). (1987). *Sleep and its disorders in children* (pp. 195–209). New York: Raven Press.

Hopkins, J., Isaacs, C., & Pitterle, P. (1995). A developmental approach to sleep problems in toddlers. In C. E. Schaefer (Ed.), *Clinical handbook of sleep disorders in children* (pp. 104, 111–113). New York: Aronson.

Kahn, A., Dan, B., Groswasser, J., Franco, P., & Sottiaux, M. (1996). Normal sleep architecture in infants and children. *Journal of Clinical Neuropsychology, 13*(3), 184–197.

Kaplan, H. I., Saddock, B. J., & Grebb, J. A. (1994). Chronobiology: The brain and behavior. In H. I. Kaplan & B. J. Saddock (Eds.), *Kaplan and Saddock's Synopsis of Psychiatry, Behavioral Sciences, and Clinical Psychiatry* (7th ed., p. 146). Baltimore: Williams & Wilkins.

Lozoff, B., Ashew, G. L., Wolf, A. L. (1996). Cosleeping and early childhood sleep problems: Effects of ethnicity and socioeconomic status. *Developmental and Behavioral Pediatrics, 7*(1), 9–10.

Minde, K., Taucon, A., & Falkner, S. (1994). *Journal of the American Academy of Child and Adolescent Psychology, 33*(8), 1114.

Palasti, S., & Potsic, W. P. (1995). Managing the child with obstructive sleep apnea. In C. E. Schaefer (Ed.), *Clinical handbook of sleep disorders in children* (p. 254). Northvale, NJ: Aronson.

Parents and children sleeping together: Cosleeping prevalence and concern. (1995). *American Journal of Orthopsychiatry, 65*(3), 411–412.

Rosen, G., Makowald, M. W., & Ferber, R. (1995). Sleep walking, confusional arousals, and sleep terrors in the child. In R. Ferber & M. Kryger, *Principal and practice of sleep medicine in the child* (p. 101). Philadelphia: Saunders.

Sadeh, A., & Anders, T. F. (1993). Sleep disorders. In C. H. Zeanah (Ed.), *Handbook of Infant Mental Health* (pp. 305–314). New York, Guilford Press.

Sheldon, S. H. (1996). *Evaluating sleep in infants and children.* Philadelphia: Lippincott.

4

TOILET TRAINING, ENURESIS, AND ENCOPRESIS

Margo Thienemann

Toilet training is a preschool task. When it goes well, children learn bladder and bowel control without their parents' battling, pressuring, shaming, or making them anxious. Unfortunately, some families struggle over issues of control and autonomy. These parents and children clash and feel frustrated, angry, and ashamed in relation to toilet training.

In the past, experts believed that difficult toilet training caused character problems. It is more likely that toilet training is one of many areas where parent and child interaction and temperamental compatibility can influence character development.

I find that all parents of preschoolers have opinions and questions about toilet training. In this chapter, I briefly review two very different methods of toilet training and provide some toilet training do's and don'ts. Then I describe two disorders that may occur when toilet training in the preschool years is *not* achieved or maintained: enuresis and encopresis.

TOILET TRAINING

From the child's point of view, the purpose of toilet training is incomprehensible. The child must stop whatever he is doing; squeeze his bottom tightly; hurry to the toilet; sit on a large, high, noisy hole filled with water; and then let urine and feces go out of his body into the hole. What a lot of effort when he could have just used his diaper! When he does this procedure right, his parents are pleased but odd: they act as if he has given them a nice present, but then say, "It's icky! Don't touch it!" and flush it away. When he takes off his pants and urinates into a pail or the floor register, or flushes other objects down the toilet, his parents are not pleased. This must be a guessing game. Anyway, when he does it right, he feels like a winner: a big boy.

Parents of different cultures, times, and families train their children with different methods, and those methods change with the times. Some parents put their children onto the potty as soon as the child can sit up and expect children to have complete bowel control by the age of nine months. Usually children introduced to the toilet this way will be disinclined to use the toilet once they can move about on their own. More parents wait until their child appears interested before beginning training, at about age two and a half. Surprisingly, families have little experimentally validated evidence to guide them. Most advice comes from parents and friends.

Methods

I will describe two effective methods tested in large samples of children: the child-oriented approach and toilet training in a day. I think you will appreciate their differences.

The Child-Oriented Approach. T. Barry Brazelton, a developmental pediatrician, introduced a child-oriented approach to toilet training. It holds that children can be trained when *they* dictate the pace because children want to please and imitate their parents, master their own impulses, and become autonomous. When *parents* set too rapid a pace, training backfires, with the child displaying defiance around toilet training and elsewhere.

Brazelton coaches parents to introduce toilet training with a relaxed and nonpressured attitude when children between eighteen and thirty months show interest in the toilet. The potty chair is placed in a prominent play area. The child is instructed, in a low-key way, in behaviors that more and more closely approximate independent toileting. When the need appears, the parent suggests that the child might try using the potty. The child progresses at his own pace, from using his chair clothed and diapered, to using it while running around with no pants on, to taking down his own pants and using the potty. Successful attempts are praised.

Using his approach, 81 percent of upper-middle-class children were dry in the daytime by age two and a half years and 98 percent were dry day and night by age five years. The child-centered method is effective and certainly avoids control struggles. Some parents cannot easily delay or surrender control of toilet training and find this method unsuitable. Others demand so little from their preschooler that they set him up for embarrassment and rob him of a sense of accomplishment.

One-Day Toilet Training. Two behavioral psychologists, Foxx and Azrin, extended a method successful with incontinent adults to children. The method, which works best when supported by trained instructors, is based on modeling and operant conditioning. The child, who has met readiness criteria at about age twenty months, is placed in a distraction-free area and is shown how a wetting doll uses a potty. The child is encouraged to drink fluids liberally. The instructor gives social (praise, kisses, hugs) or edible reinforcements each time the child indicates a need to go to the potty, gets the potty out, removes her pants, and passes urine. If she wets, the child is reprimanded, given a time-out, and required to change her own pants.

This method was reported to be a little more effective than the child-oriented approach. It is much quicker and has been useful in developmentally delayed individuals. However, some children become remarkably oppositional and given to tantrum. Parents at risk for child abuse are recommended not to use this method. Harsh training or punishment for failure produces unwanted emotional effects and can backfire.

Toilet Training Do's and Don'ts

What method should you recommend to your clients? I recommend toilet training that combines the relaxed child-paced style of Brazelton with the reinforcements of Foxx and Azrin, along with expressions of mild disappointment for accidents and communication of future expectations. When efforts in training are accompanied with regressed or defiant behaviors, then toilet training efforts should be relaxed for a time.

Children with family histories of bed wetting should begin toilet training early (at age twelve to fifteen months) because early efforts decrease the incidence of later wetting. Beginning training after twenty months in these children may increase the incidence of enuresis. Well-timed, intensive toilet training with positive praise and reinforcement and mild disapproval for failures helps children become continent.

Toilet Training Do's

1. Do wait until the child is interested, is physically able to get to the toilet, can pull down his pants, indicates the need to go, and can follow directions. Then wait a few months more. Children may show interest in the toilet before they are actually ready for toilet training. Usually they are ready after they are age two or two and a half.
2. Do allow the child to go without diapers as much as possible during training.
3. Do reward the child for efforts with low-key praise or a small reinforcement, such as a sticker, bit of "potty candy," or marshmallow.
4. Do reprimand the child very *mildly* when he has an accident. "I don't like it when you tinkle on the floor."

5. Do communicate to the child that you are confident that he eventually will be able to go to the toilet like a big child. "Maybe next time you will go to the toilet. I would like that. You could go to the potty like a big girl [or Mommy]."

6. Do provide opportunities for your child to learn from modeling, by parents, siblings, peers, characters in books, and videos. Examples motivate and help the child learn

Toilet Training Don'ts

1. Do not rush to the toilet when he needs to go. He will associate toileting with worry.

2. Do not shame the child for accidents or for wearing diapers.

3. Do not begin toilet training when you and your child are in the midst of many control struggles.

4. Do not awaken the child in the night to go to the bathroom. You are not helping him learn to get up.

5. Do not begin toilet training at a time of stress for the child (birth of a sibling, moving to a new house, starting a preschool, during a divorce, when a parent is hospitalized).

6. Do not begin toilet training at a time the child is tackling other developmental tasks (learning to walk).

7. Do not forget that toilet training is a gradual process. Some children need help wiping themselves after a bowel movement even when they are five years old.

8. Do not wrestle for control with the child. Understand that children need to feel in control. Respect that in a real way.

ENURESIS AND ENCOPRESIS

The preschooler lays the groundwork for maintaining bladder and bowel control. Preschool years are the best time for prevention and identification of toileting problems. When children past preschool age are incontinent of urine, they have *enuresis*.

When children defecate in inappropriate places, the problem is called *encopresis*. Of the 5 to 7 million children in this country who have enuresis or encopresis, most have recently begun school.

Enuresis and encopresis, which burden, embarrass, and frustrate children and their families, are two of the most common reasons parents consult primary care physicians. Although they are most commonly treated in the primary care setting, mental health workers play an important part in treating and preventing these disorders. When toilet training is going poorly, we work with families to prevent later problems. We identify, support, and educate children and families in trouble and guide them through treatment. We address psychodynamic and systemic issues that interfere with progress. In this chapter, I provide information I hope you will find helpful in treating the enuretic and encopretic children in your practice. I begin with an example of Toby, a boy who had both enuresis and encopresis.

T O B Y

Toby is a five-year-old boy who complained that his friends shunned him. Over the last year, Toby had begun to soil his pants and wet his bed. His friends called him "stinky" and declined play dates.

Toby soiled his underwear with smudged or formed feces about once per week. Three times per week, Toby wet his bed. Toby was constipated and said that having a bowel movement was painful. When he was busy, he did not "remember" to go to the toilet. Toby felt ashamed and thought that his family was getting frustrated with him. In fact, they were.

Toby's mother reported that she had taken a relaxed approach to toilet training. She began when Toby was two, soon after his brother was born. Because she was very busy with the baby, she remembered little about the training except that Toby was not interested in sitting on the toilet very long, even when she read to him. By the time he was three, he used the toilet pretty consistently.

Toby was a bright, active kindergartner. He played elaborate games of pirates and space men with his several close friends or his three-year-old brother. He did not interrupt these games to go to the bathroom, nor did he stop playing if he soiled. Toby's mother usually needed to ask him several times to comply with anything. She had some success with star charts and time-outs.

Our clinical interview found no psychiatric illness, trauma, sexual abuse, or significant family history. A possible link was made between the onset of symptoms and Toby's entry into preschool. I postulated that the stress of his brother's birth during Toby's toilet training may have contributed to the development of his current problems.

I referred Toby to his pediatrician. She found no abnormality on physical, neurological, or laboratory examination with the exception of a large amount of hard stool in his rectum. She diagnosed encopresis resulting from chronic constipation and felt that the wetting was likely secondary to the constipation. She explained to Toby the mechanisms involved in encopresis and enuresis. She explained how the phenomenon of sensory fatigue prevented *him* from noticing his smell, when others could.

She recommended therapies to clean out his bowel, then a program to prevent him from becoming constipated again. The program combined behavior training with mild cathartics and a high-fiber diet.

We coordinated our work with the pediatrician. Toby, his parents, and I developed star charts to track and reinforce visits to the toilet, taking medication, eating prescribed foods, and dry nights. We worked out strategies for Toby to excuse himself from play or class to go to the bathroom. We tempered disappointments about setbacks and helped Toby with his feelings of shame.

Within three months, the frequency of Toby's wetting and soiling had greatly diminished. He continued to visit his pediatrician to monitor medication and visit me to enforce behavior interventions and deal with the rare relapses. Toby was relieved and proud of his accomplishment. He invited friends over for successful play dates.

ENURESIS

Enuresis is the most common elimination problem in late preschool- and school-age children.

Definition and Epidemiology

Enuresis is defined in *DSM-IV* as repeated voluntary or involuntary voiding of urine into bed or clothes at least twice per week for at least three consecutive months or causing clinically significant distress or impairment in social, academic, or other important areas of functioning in a child at least five years old (or equivalent developmental level) that is not due exclusively to the direct physiological effect of a substance (for example, a diuretic) or a general medical condition (for example, diabetes, spina bifida, a seizure disorder).

Enuresis is specified as nocturnal (during sleep) only, diurnal (while awake) only, or nocturnal and diurnal. A child who never consistently achieves dryness has primary enuresis. When the child wets after dryness had been achieved for at least three to six months, he has secondary enuresis.

Enuresis is common in small children and rare in older adolescents. In a community sample, the prevalence of enuresis ranged from 26 percent and 17 percent of, respectively, six-year-old boys and girls to 2 percent and 1 percent of, respectively, seventeen-year-old boys and girls. Fifteen percent of children of each age group stop wetting each year. Although it usually resolves spontaneously, enuresis deserves intervention. If children are still wetting after they are four years old, they are more likely to continue wetting and develop other difficulties.

Demographic factors affect the frequency of enuresis. Male sex, later birth order, and larger family size are generally thought to be associated with enuresis. Some investigators, but not others, include lower socioeconomic status, lower height, lower bone age, and later age of sexual maturity as risk factors.

Etiology

The specific cause of many cases of enuresis is unknown. Toilet training, heredity, developmental disorders, sleep and psychiatric disorders, environmental stressors, and medical problems are all causes of enuresis. It is likely that a number of these factors interact to cause enuresis in any one case.

Toilet Training. Difficulties in toilet training sometimes cause enuresis. When stressful events such as repeated hospitalization, separations from primary caretakers, or family break-ups interrupt toilet training, enuresis is more common. If a child is tackling new milestones or is having emotional or behavioral problems at the same time he is toilet training, he is more likely to develop enuresis. The match between the child's developmental readiness and temperament, parental training attitudes and methods, and environmental milieu are important to the child's experience and success of training.

Heredity. Enuresis is inherited in about 75 percent of cases. Danish investigators have recently identified an enuresis gene. If parents wet when they were young, it is very likely that their children will.

Developmental Disorders. As a group, enuretic children develop and mature a little later than other children. Specific abilities must develop for children to go to the toilet independently. To achieve bladder control, the child must be able to be aware of bladder fullness, retain urine voluntarily, and start and stop the flow of urine at any bladder fullness. Children develop these abilities at different rates, usually between the ages of one and five.

To toilet independently, a child must also be able to walk, stoop, pull down pants, sit still, have adequate language, and be willing to follow instructions. The fact that, on the whole, boys mature later than girls may explain the fact that twice as many boys as girls are enuretic.

Sleep Disorder. Some parents believe that their children wet because they sleep so deeply. Sleep studies have not borne this out. Not only do enuretic and nonenuretic children spend the same amount of the night in deepest sleep, wetting occurs equally in any stage of sleep.

Psychiatric Disorder. Although children who wet have a higher incidence of psychiatric disorders, behavior disturbances, and learning disabilities than the general child population, no characteristic disorder goes along with or causes enuresis. Rather, problems coexist. Only when a behavior disturbance results from the child or his environment's reaction to enuresis does treatment of one condition affect the other. On the whole, adolescents who were enuretic children are well adjusted.

Stressors. Enuresis is more common when children have experienced a number of stressors during the time of toilet training. An environmental change, especially one that causes increased anxiety in already nervous children, can cause secondary enuresis. Enuresis can be a symptom of sexual abuse of boys or girls.

Organic Disorders. Although attainment of bladder control requires the coordination of complex neurological and endocrine signals, renal function, and voluntary and involuntary muscular control, less than 1 percent of enuresis has an organic cause. Research has found two functional contributors to enuresis. In some children with enuresis, the bladder does not hold as much urine because it contracts before the bladder is full. This problem is termed *decreased functional bladder capacity.*

Some children have abnormalities of antidiuretic hormone (ADH) function. ADH is a hormone secreted by the pituitary to signal to the body, among other things, "Hold onto fluids. Do not let water out into the urine." Under ADH influence, a smaller amount of more concentrated urine is produced. Some enuretic children do not secrete ADH with a normal daily rhythm. In others, hormone receptors may not be appropriately sensitive. With inadequate ADH action, children produce excessive, dilute urine and are prone to wet.

Dynamic, structural, and infectious problems in the urinary tract may cause enuresis, but they do so infrequently. Disorders of the nervous system, such as meningomyelocele and spina bifida, cause enuresis. When the kidneys cannot adequately concentrate urine in diabetes mellitus, diabetes insipidus, or sickle cell anemia, enuresis may result. Urinary tract infections, which often cause painful and frequent urination, may also cause enuresis.

Evaluation

Ninety-nine percent of children stop wetting by age seventeen. Nature cures almost all enuresis eventually, but often with an unacceptable social and emotional toll. The hassle, shame, and stress of enuresis warrant evaluation and at least supportive and educational treatment. In this section, I describe how I evaluate a child who wets and then discuss treatments.

I begin the evaluation with a careful history. I want to know the pattern of wetting: its frequency, timing, setting, and whether enuresis is associated with any particular stressor for the child or family. I ask the family how they have managed the problem. We review the history of toilet training, paying attention to the method, timing, concomitant stressors, child's reaction, and parents' experience. I examine the toll that enuresis has taken on the child and the rest of the family emotionally, socially, and in daily life. I ask what each family member believes causes the enuresis and about any family history of enuresis. I do a complete psychiatric interview and mental status examination, seeing the family together and the parents and children separately. That way I can observe possible systemic difficulties, understand different family members' reactions to the problem in private, and assess for evidence of precipitating trauma, stressors, and other psychopathology.

I take a brief medical history, but I always refer my patient to the primary care physician for medical evaluation. The physician

will take a detailed medical history, do a physical and neurological examination, and order urinalysis and other tests if indicated
by history and physical. It is likely that the physician will watch
the child urinate. The characteristics of the urine stream and the
child's control over urination will help the physician eliminate
organic causes for the wetting.

Treatment

Education, behavioral interventions, hypnosis, medication, and
adjunctive psychotherapies are all possible components of treatment. Each patient requires a customized combination. Therapies provided by nonphysicians play an important role in the
treatment of both enuresis and encopresis.

Because of managed care, treatment of these conditions frequently falls to the physician. If you receive a referral, you will
need to work closely with the child's primary care physician, who
may need your help in justifying why you, in particular, need to
be involved in treatment, especially if you are "out of plan." Possible reasons to use you may include relevant expertise, long-
standing relationships with the family, and physical logistics. In
designing your treatment plan, you will have to ensure that all
aspects of care (individual, behavioral, collateral, and family therapies as indicated) are included in the plan. You will have to educate reviewers that nonpharmacologic treatment is often
first-line and other nonmedical treatments are necessary, as well.
Therapy always starts with education—these days, sometimes
first to the third parties.

Education. The longer I am a therapist, the more I appreciate
the role that education plays in improving the patient's experience of his symptoms. We cannot often know the exact reason a
child is enuretic, but we can explain possible contributors, and
the methods and rationales of successful treatment. We can help
children and parents understand that the enuretic child is not at
fault. With information, enuresis will be more tolerable, and the
patient and family are more likely to be allies in treatment.

Behavior Therapy. Behavior therapies are the safest and most effective treatments for enuresis. Because these therapies require more therapist and family commitment than does medication therapy, they are too often overlooked. They should not be.

Alarm systems are the most effective and longest lasting of enuresis therapies. Because these systems require family participation and commitment, the therapist's support and expertise can make the difference between success and continued wetting. Seventy-five to 90 percent of children will stop wetting on the first trial with an alarm system. A second trial in the small proportion of children who relapse is equally effective. Alarm therapy failure is usually due to inconsistent cooperation or failure to use the alarm properly. Continued, regular contacts with a health care provider improve the chances for success.

Modern alarm systems usually consist of a clip-on moisture sensor that attaches to the child's pajamas. Alarm systems are safe and inexpensive (they range from forty to eighty dollars) and available from medical supply companies. The following story about Rhesa explains alarm system use.

RHESA

Rhesa was a six-year-old girl I treated for Obsessive-Compulsive Disorder. Rhesa wet her bed several times each week, as had her mother until she was eleven. Rhesa was not *very* ashamed about wetting, but she was tired of having to change her sheets and reluctant to sleep at a friend's house. Psychiatric and physical examination revealed no additional concerns. We started a bed-wetting diary and elected to try an alarm system.

I instructed Rhesa and her mother how the alarm system works. When Rhesa begins to wet, the alarm makes a noise. Rhesa awakens fully (or her parent awakens her), turns off the alarm, and hurries to the bathroom to finish urinating in the toilet. Rhesa turns on the alarm again and goes back to bed. I explained that Rhesa would soon learn to awaken by herself when she needed to, or, more likely, she would sleep dry through the night.

Rhesa practiced turning off the alarm. Her mother agreed to sleep in Rhesa's extra bed so as to be available and supportive. They put a night light in Rhesa's room. Because she did not wet every night, we had Rhesa drink soft drinks before bed, so that she would be more likely to use the alarm.

Rhesa and her mother used the alarm faithfully and recorded her wet and dry nights. We met weekly and reviewed the diary. Rhesa's mother and I praised her for her efforts, and I reinforced her mother's involvement. During the second week of using the alarm, Rhesa woke up by herself twice to go to the toilet. By the end of a month, Rhesa had six consecutive dry nights without the alarm's going off.

When Rhesa had had fourteen straight dry nights, she wanted to try sleeping without the alarm. She stayed dry for several months, then wet her bed after moving into a new house. Using the alarm and diary, she was dry within a month and confident enough to go to camp.

Bladder training can increase the child's ability to hold urine. Because many children with enuresis have a decreased functional bladder capacity, a technique called *retention training* is sometimes recommended. Children are trained to hold their urine as long as they can and to practice stopping and starting their urine stream. I do not recommend this type of training in a child who is not enthusiastic about trying it. It could intensify control struggles. However, this method may be helpful in willing children.

Dry bed training is an effective and intense program based on the idea that enuresis is a learning problem. Dry bed training combines the use of the urine alarm and retention training with a toilet training procedure developed by Azrin and Foxx. Normal, autistic, and mentally retarded enuretic children can respond within one night.

An instructor trains the child. First, the child practices getting up and going to the toilet twenty times just before bedtime. At bedtime, the child drinks fluids and goes to bed with an alarm. Each hour, the child is awakened, walks to the bathroom door, and is asked whether he could delay urination for an hour. If the child cannot delay urination, he uses the toilet, is praised, and returns to bed. If the child can wait, he is praised and returns to bed. At the bed, the child is praised for the bed's dryness, given more fluids, and sent to sleep for another hour.

If the child wets, the trainer turns off the alarm, awakens and reprimands the child, and sends the child to the bathroom to finish urinating. The child must then change his clothes and sheets and practice getting up and going to the toilet twenty more times before going back to sleep for an hour.

The second night, if the child wet the night before, he practices going to the toilet twenty times before bed. The alarm is set, and the child sleeps until his parents awaken him at their bedtime to go to the toilet. The reinforcements and consequences are continued as they were the night before. When dryness is achieved, parents and relatives praise the child. After a dry week, the alarm is removed.

Hypnosis is an effective and long-lasting treatment for enuresis, especially for children older than seven years old. Hypnosis can work in as few as four to six sessions. It has no negative side effects, and because hypnosis gives the child a skill and power to help himself, it can help build self-esteem. The child must be motivated to practice prescribed self-hypnosis exercises regularly. Trent was a boy with whom hypnosis was successful after medication failed.

TRENT

Trent, an eight year old who had had diurnal and nocturnal enuresis until age seven, still wet his bed about three nights per week. Many family members had suffered from enuresis too. Trent's self-esteem was low, and he feared camping with his scout troop. After ruling out medical reasons for enuresis and an only slightly successful trial of a medication called desmopressin, Trent's pediatrician referred him for a trial of hypnosis.

Trent felt that listening to motivational tapes had helped him in tennis and was excited to try hypnosis. The therapist in the clinic taught Trent that his mind has power over his bladder. She taught him to hypnotize himself, inducing a trance by thinking of his favorite place. She suggested that Trent is capable of dealing effectively with his problems. He will hold the urine when his bladder is full until he is fully awake, then get up from a dry bed, walk to the bathroom, urinate in the toilet, and return to sleep in the nice dry bed.

Trent was instructed to keep a diary and practice self-hypnosis two to three times per day. He returned weekly for hypnosis, self-hypnosis training, and review of the diary and reinforcement. Within two months, Trent was wetting only once per week. He could trace most wetting to having missed a couple of days of self-hypnosis. His therapist noted that his self-confidence and sense of mastery had improved and that he felt happier.

Medication. Medication is used more commonly than are the more effective nonpharmacological interventions. In the short run, it may seem easier to prescribe or take medication. However, medication risks side effects and may not give children (and parents) the success, skills, and sense of accomplishment that successful behavior or hypnotic therapy will. I believe that medication is most helpful as an adjunct to behavior therapies that have not helped enough.

Desmopressin (DDAVP) is a relatively new synthetic form of ADH, which comes as a nasal spray. When children with enuresis take DDAVP in the evening, they produce a smaller volume of urine overnight. About one-fourth of children become dry during short-term treatment with DDAVP, but 95 percent relapse when the medication is discontinued. Children who wet about four times per week can expect to reduce the frequency by about one-third while taking the medication. Side effects are usually mild and can include headaches, nosebleeds, stuffy nose, and mild abdominal pain. Some children have suffered from seizures as a result of DDAVP therapy. Until more information is available about the seizures and long-term side effects, and because of the lower efficacy and usual relapse with DDAVP, I do not recommend this medication as a first choice of therapy.

Imipramine is an antidepressant that has been used for many years as a moderately effective treatment for enuresis. The mechanism by which imipramine works in enuresis is not known. As with DDAVP, when imipramine is discontinued, enuresis usually resumes. Imipramine can be fatal in overdose, demonstrates wildly varying serum levels at any dosage, and occasionally has uncomfortable side effects. I do not recommend imipramine as the first treatment of choice for enuretics. I have used it successfully in combination with behavior methods when these methods alone failed.

Counseling and Psychotherapy. Traditional psychotherapy alone does not reduce bed wetting. Psychotherapists improve treatment outcome when they understand behavior therapy; educate, motivate, and emotionally support patients and their families; and troubleshoot when therapy flags. Either working alone or in conjunction with the primary care staff, the therapist is uniquely skilled in helping the family to accept and support the child. The therapist can help the child work through shame and anger, instill optimism, and help the child assume responsibility for his part in the success of the treatment. When serious psychiatric conditions coexist with enuresis, the therapist can help the family to decide how to allocate their energies and resources. When family issues interfere with treatment, mental health professionals can identify and address these.

ENCOPRESIS

Enuresis is usually a secret nocturnal problem. Encopresis is a daytime problem that broadcasts itself. Of the two, encopresis is more disabling, may take longer to treat, and raises more countertransference issues.

Definition and Epidemiology

Children with encopresis defecate in inappropriate places, such as their clothing or the floor. According to *DSM-IV,* soiling must occur once a month for at least three months, chronological or developmental age must be at least four, and the behavior must not be the result of a substance, such as a laxative, or from a medical condition except constipation. Ninety-five percent of cases are specified as encopresis with constipation and overflow incontinence. The remaining minority of cases are associated with acute stressors or emotional disturbance and family problems.

Encopresis occurs in about 1.5 percent of seven- and eight-year-olds and in almost no children over age sixteen. Boys outnumber girls with a ratio of about four or six to one.

Etiology

As with enuresis, multiple factors contribute to a child's developing encopresis. Causes range from chronic constipation, the most common, to rarer organic and emotionally based encopresis.

Psychosocial Factors. Psychosocial and physical factors interacting at critical stages may cause the disorder. When stressful events disrupt toilet training, training may be incomplete. When parents act wildly enthusiastic or terribly disappointed around toilet behaviors, the child may become overly preoccupied with bowel movements and be at risk for encopresis.

The bathroom can become one more battle opportunity in a family where children and their parents have conflicts over autonomy and control. If a healthy solution is not found, the child may use dysfunctional bowel control as an attempt to hold his own. Sexual abuse can cause encopresis. Anal trauma leads to painful defecation, then constipation. The child may repress anger at the molester or those who failed to protect him, then express the anger in a regressive way as encopresis.

Chronic Constipation. Children who make negative associations with defecating are more likely to hold back feces, become constipated, and have encopresis. In infancy and toddlerhood, painful associations with defecation, such as constipation or coercive medical interventions, may predispose the children to later encopresis. Young children may develop fears about falling in, monsters hiding, losing something of themselves, or having babies into the toilet. School-age children may avoid school bathrooms because of a lack of privacy or fear of ridicule. They may also be too busy to take time to go to the toilet or lack the task persistence to complete going. After painful defecation, with a large stool or diarrhea, children may fear having another painful bowel movement and hold back.

Once a child holds in feces, a chain of physiological events follows, which can cause the child to be incontinent of feces and even urine. As the rectum and lower bowel fill with feces, the body becomes less able to expel them. The overstretched muscle wall cannot contract well. The nerves that signal to the bowel muscle lose their sensitivity. As feces accumulate, water is absorbed, and the feces become larger and harder. Defecation can become difficult and painful, and the body does not appropriately signal the brain to do so. Sometimes painful anal fissures or hemorrhoids develop, compounding the difficulty. Anticipating pain, children avoid defecating, become more constipated, and develop abdominal pain. The anal sphincter becomes compromised, and mucus and soft feces leak around the impacted mass. The distended rectum presses on the bladder, decreasing the capacity, and the child may dribble urine or wet.

Soiling accidents usually happen late in the day (3:00 to 7:00 P.M.). Soiling at night is rare and a sign of poor prognosis. Bumpy bus rides and walks home are high-risk times. Because of sensory fatigue, children may not notice the smell that others do. Because the chronic constipation decreases sensory feedback in the rectum, the child may not be aware of the soiling.

Secondary Emotional Problems.   Do not assume that each case of encopresis stems from an emotional disturbance. Emotional problems secondary to encopresis are easy to confuse with causes. Children who are incontinent of feces often have poor self-esteem and depressive symptoms. They fear ridicule and withdraw socially. Frequently, encopretic children develop other somatic complaints. Whole families can become angry and con-flicted over ways to handle the problem. Bathroom habits may preoccupy everyone . Parents and siblings may see the child as lazy and dirty and blame him for his problem. The family may constrict activities to avoid embarrassing situations. These symp-toms are secondary to the encopresis. If they do not resolve with resolution of the encopresis, then further mental health inter-vention is indicated.

Organic Causes.   Rarely, a medical condition other than con-stipation causes encopresis. The pediatrician will evaluate encopretic children to rule out Hirschsprung's disease, hypothy-roidism, hyperparathyroidism, parasites, inflammatory bowel dis-ease, spinal cord disorders, muscular disorders, and anorectal lesions.

Encopresis without Constipation or Other Organic Cause. Some children with good bowel control nevertheless defecate in their clothes or other places. Emotional problems cause this type of encopresis. Encopresis caused by constipation or organic dis-orders is treated in the medical setting. These other cases fall into the realm of the mental health professional.

Encopresis Which Is Similar to an Adjustment Disorder.   Chil-dren who "purposely" soil may be responding to a acute and stressful event. This type of encopresis is much like an adjust-ment disorder, which occurs in response to entry to school, sep-aration from primary caregivers, hospitalization, or the birth of a new sibling.

Encopresis with More Serious Psychopathology. More challenging are encopretic children who defecate in a seemingly
punitive way or smear feces while overtly denying that they are
doing so. These children, typically older than those with constipation, have severe family problems and psychopathology.
They are usually covertly angry, and their families are chronically contentious and unstable. As you may imagine, families
become quite angry at these children for their offensive behavior. In families who already have trouble coping, the anger can
spiral dangerously, children soil even more, and the family situation deteriorates further.

Evaluation

As with enuresis, evaluation is best accomplished by a well-coor-
dinated effort between mental health and medical therapists.

Mental Health Evaluation. I evaluate encopresis in much the
same way as I do enuresis. I get a baseline knowledge of the patterns of soiling. I assess the child's current toilet habits for avoidance of, opportunities for, and setting of defecation. I determine
the severity and frequency of encopresis and ask the family to
begin a diary of events and elimination.

I inquire about the onset of encopresis and associated stressors. We review the timing, method, and conflicts of toilet training; the timing of critical life events in development; and the
contributions to and reactions of the child's environment to the
problem

Next, I try to find out what has been the toll and what may be
the secondary gain for the symptom. I am interested in what the
child and family each think has caused encopresis. I note whether
the family agrees on coping strategies and what those have been.

I try to determine whether there are factors in the child, such
as depression, social problems, attention problems, learning
problems, or retardation, that aggravate the encopresis. I try to

find out whether family strife, sibling conflicts, marital instability, financial setbacks, or deprivation drive or worsen the condition. I meet with the family as a whole, with the caretakers alone, and with the child alone. I can see family interactions and observe private and candid reactions to the problem.

Medical Evaluation.   As in the evaluation of enuresis, I always refer the family to a primary care physician, who will perform physical and neurological exams, and sometimes X-ray the abdomen. When the history and physical examination suggest a medical problem, the doctor may order laboratory tests or refer the child to a specialist.

Treatment

Different types of encopresis require different interventions. I will describe the ways medical and mental health professionals address the different problems.

Encopresis with Incomplete Toilet Training or in Response to an Acute Stressor.   When a young child has never achieved bowel continence or regresses in response to an acute stressor, simple behavioral interventions are usually adequate. Parents make sure that the child takes in an adequate amount of fluids and fiber. The child sits on the toilet for five to ten minutes after meals to take advantage of the gastrocolic reflex, which stimulates defecation when the stomach fills. Reinforcers, such as reading to the child while she is on the toilet, mild praise, and star charts with rewards add incentive and improve success. Usually with this sort of intervention, this is a short-lived problem.

Encopresis with Constipation and Overflow Soiling.   Toby, the boy described in the first case, had encopresis because of constipation and overflow soiling. Toby's treatment was typical, but his course was shorter than that of some other children, which may take months to years until constipation and soiling resolve.

To begin treatment, we educated Toby and his parents about the mechanics of constipation and how it causes soiling. We applauded Toby's family for not blaming him. After explaining the treatment program, we felt confident that, with the support of the primary care physician and our help, the family could carry it out. If we had not had that confidence or if fecal retention had been severe, we would have admitted Toby to the hospital. There, his bowel "clean- out" and establishment of the maintenance phase of treatment could have been started and taught under supervision. (Children are also hospitalized when outpatient efforts fail or parent-child problems make it inadvisable to have the parents administer the treatment.)

The pediatrician supervised the bowel clean-out. Toby received two enemas at home on the first day, a rectal suppository the second, and an oral stool softener the next. He had to repeat this cycle again for full disimpaction, because X-ray showed excessive feces remaining in his colon. The pediatrician wanted to be sure that treatment was not sabotaged by incompleteness at this stage. Toby knew, after this, that the worst was over.

Toby and his mother bought a kitchen timer, some new books, and some bran cereal for the maintenance phase. In this phase, Toby and his body learned to keep regular bowel habits. Twice a day, after high-fiber meals, Toby would sit on the toilet for ten timed minutes and read. He earned a star for sitting and another for having a bowel movement. He earned another star for taking his mineral oil and vitamins. We did not reward clean pants because we did not want to encourage Toby to hold bowel movements in and avoid going to the toilet. It was hard for Toby to sit there so long, but the thought of earning new computer games made it easier. Mixing the mineral oil in a soft drink helped too.

I met with Toby alone and with his mother weekly and spoke with his pediatrician after these meetings. In our sessions, I reviewed the star charts and praised both Toby and his mother for compliance and effort. When Toby had trouble with compliance, we retailored the reinforcers to be more immediate and attractive.

As Toby progressed, the pediatrician adjusted the mineral oil and vitamin dosage, and we tightened up on the reward schedule. When things got harder, she prescribed mild laxatives, and we loosened up on reinforcers. After a few months, Toby got into a habit of eating and toileting, and his bowels responded.

Because Toby had had problems with encopresis at school, we made arrangements, with his permission, for him to use a private bathroom there. We practiced having Toby excuse himself from class. The teachers gave him as-needed bathroom privileges, and Toby brought extra clothes to school. Until his bowel function was regularized, Toby's mother picked him up from school, to avoid embarrassing accidents on the bouncy bus.

Encopresis Without Constipation, with Emotional Problems. Now comes the most difficult treatment of the chapter. I will never forget the first inpatient case of my training, and not only because it was first. I will describe the case to illustrate methods and some the challenges of treating a "willfully" soiling child.

MISSY

Missy was a ten-year-old encopretic girl who was admitted to the psychosomatic unit after having been treated unsuccessfully in the gastroenterology clinic for six months. Missy was defecating in her pants almost every day. Her physicians felt that emotional and family problems were the most important cause of encopresis.

Missy had most of her "accidents" at home. She usually denied having soiled and hid her soiled underwear. She did not want to take mineral oil and resented efforts to make her sit on the toilet or do her laundry.

Missy was the youngest, by eight years, of three children. Her mother died when Missy was less than a year old. She was raised by her father, Jackson, who was an abstract sculptor, her two older brothers, and Maria, a live-out sitter who had worked with the family all of Missy's life. Her care was loving and consistent, and she was securely attached to her father, siblings, and sitter. Missy, the family's darling baby, was toilet trained and disciplined in a permissive manner. Her father and brothers were easygoing and gave in to her occasional tantrums.

Two years before the hospital admission, Jackson fell in love with an accountant. After a year, they became engaged, and Lilian moved in with the family. Lilian, anxious to be accepted as a competent parent, was not as easygoing as Missy's family. She explained to Missy's father that giving in to Missy's tantrums would not help Missy and pointed out that Missy needed to take more responsibility. In general, Lilian tightened up the ship.

It had been hard for Missy to have her father going on dates, but to have Lilian in her home and in her face was just too much. Missy became pouty, petulant, and passive. Before long, she was encopretic. No one in the household liked the symptom, and Lilian and Missy tangled over it.

In the hospital, we began a coordinated team effort. Missy continued on the program of mineral oil and behavior modification prescribed by the medical service. She underwent psychological testing, began family evaluation and treatment with a social worker, and started seeing me for individual therapy.

In the milieu, Missy interacted little with peers. Psychological testing and figure drawing revealed no evidence of sexual abuse or other major psychopathology. The family therapist met with each family member to determine their attitudes toward and reactions to the problem. She helped them talk about their frustration and anger toward Missy and explored the way Jackson and Lilian differed in parenting styles. When the family met together and discussed the difficulties involved in incorporating a new person into the family, Missy was silent.

Individual therapy provided me lessons in patience and countertransference. Missy came willingly to my office but would not say a word except a rare, "Can I go now?" I tried everything I could think of and everything my supervisors suggested. I offered to play cards, checkers, the squiggle game. I offered her the blackboard. I asked her questions. I talked about the confidentiality of our sessions. I spoke about the way I imagined she might be experiencing her family troubles, her plight of having to be in the hospital, having to take mineral oil, and having to sit in the little office with me for an hour every day. Some days, the little office was smelly. I told her that I believed that she was communicating with me in a special way that worked by making me feel the way she does much of the time: angry, frustrated, and helpless to change anything. I thought she worried about losing her father to Lilian, resented Lilian's intruding into the family and taking charge, and felt powerless to get Lilian out. She still did not speak, but over the course of the treatment, I did not notice the smell as frequently.

Missy began to soil a little less often, but Lilian was frustrated by the slow pace of improvement and Missy's seeming nonparticipation in therapy. She was uncomfortable when the focus of the therapy was on her reasonable discipline or new position in the family. She and Jackson withdrew Missy from the hospital before we recommended discharge.

I was surprised, about a year and a half later, to run into Missy outside my office. She acted friendly and said that she wanted me to meet her girlfriend. I asked her how things were going. She replied, "Fine," and added that her father had not gotten married after all.

I wondered what would have happened if Missy and her family had been able to stick with the therapy. I hoped that somehow Missy had learned ways to be assertive and deal with her anger verbally and directly.

Countertransference Issues. Therapy with children like Missy is packed with challenging countertransference issues. When a child withholds interaction, you feel challenged to try harder, be creative, and reach out to this child. Later, you may feel angry and frustrated, then powerless, inept, and hopeless. Boredom may beckon as a good defense, and you may be tempted to terminate the sessions or pick up a book.

You then must truly wrestle with your feelings (and senses) to maintain an empathetic and therapeutic stance. You must remember the principle of projective identification, by which, as Missy did, the patient makes the therapist feel as powerless as she. You must remember that the child is silently and desperately clenching onto power in the session and therapeutic relationship. The child does so at the expense of enjoying an interaction with a warm, interested adult who is not repulsed by the child and respects her need for control. You must gently model for the patient ways to express feelings *verbally*. You must maintain an atmosphere where the child will feel safe enough to surrender some of the little control she feels she has. You must carefully walk the line between the confidentiality of the tenuous relationship and the need to coordinate closely with the treatment team. You must help the child by endorsing her cooperation with possibly invasive and controlling medical and behavior interventions while helping her find aspects of her life she can control without such a cost. Because of the difficulty of the problem and the countertransference issues raised, I find this work strenuous, educating, and ultimately rewarding.

Treatment Outcome

Encopresis is often a chronic problem. About half of all children with encopresis associated with constipation are cured after one year. Two to seven years later, approximately 70 percent of encopresis has resolved. Good treatment compliance and the child's sense that his efforts will be effective (an internal locus of control) predict a good outcome. If a long period of time has elapsed before treatment begins, resolution will take longer.

Enuresis and encopresis are two socially unacceptable, frustrating, and embarrassing problems of late preschool- and school-age children. In the majority of cases, developmental events, stressors, and genetic or physiological factors interact to cause them. Usually the problems respond to medical and behavior interventions coordinated by the primary care physician and the mental health worker. The minority of cases will require more intensive intervention with the addition of family and pharmacological therapy. A knowledge of the causes and treatments of these conditions and awareness of countertransference will speed effective therapy.

NOTES

P. 83, *When it goes well, . . . or making them anxious:* Fraiberg, S. H. (1959). *The magic years.* New York: Scribner, pp. 91–102.

P. 83, *In the past, experts believed . . . caused character problems:* Marans, S., & Cohen, D. J. (1991). Child psychoanalytic theories of development. In M. Lewis (Ed.), *Child and adolescent psychiatry,* pp. 129–145.

P. 84, *More parents wait until their child appears interested:* Bloom, D. A., Seeley, W. W., Ritchey, M. L., & McGuire, E. J. (1993). Toilet habits and continence in children: An opportunity sampling in search of normal parameters. *Journal of Urology, 149*(5), 1087–1090.

P. 84, *T. Berry Brazelton, a developmental pediatrician:* Brazelton, T. B. (1962). A child-oriented approach to toilet training. *Pediatrics, 29,* 121–128.

P. 85, *Two behavioral psychologists, Foxx and Azrin:* Foxx, A. Z. (1985). The successful treatment of diurnal and nocturnal enuresis and encopresis. *Child and Family Behavior Medicine, 7,* 39–47.

P. 88, *Enuresis and encopresis, which burden, embarrass, and frustrate children and their families:* Miller, K. (1993). Concomitant nonpharmacologic therapy in the treatment of primary nocturnal enuresis [Special edition]. *Clinical Pediatrics,* 32–37.

P. 90, *Enuresis is defined in* DSM-IV: American Psychiatric Association. (1994). *Diagnostic and statistical manual of mental disorders* (4th ed.). Washington, DC: Author, pp. 108–110.

P. 90, *In a community sample, the prevalence of enuresis:* Gross, R. T., & Dornbusch, S. M. (1983). Disordered processes of elimination. In M. Levine, W. B. Carey, A. C. Crocker, & R. T. Gross (Eds.), *Developmental behavioral pediatrics.* Philadelphia: Saunders, p. 573.

P. 90, *Fifteen percent of children of each age group stop wetting each year:* Doleys, D. M., & Dolce, J. J. (1982). Toilet training and enuresis. *Pediatric Clinics of North America, 29*(2), 297–313.

P. 91, *Danish investigators have recently identified an enuresis gene:* Eiberg, H., Berendt, I., & Mohr, J. (1995). Assignment of dominant inherited nocturnal enuresis to chromosome 13q. *Nature Genetics, 10*(3), 354–356.

P. 92, *Sleep studies have not borne this out:* Shaffer, D. (1987). The development of bladder control. In M. Rutter (Ed.), *Developmental psychiatry,* Washington, DC: American Psychiatric Press, pp. 129–137.

P. 92, *Enuresis can be a symptom of sexual abuse of boys or girls:* Feehan, C. J. (1995). Enuresis secondary to sexual assault. *Journal of the American Academy of Child and Adolescent Psychiatry, 34*(11), 1404.

P. 92, *Some children have abnormalities of antidiuretic hormone (ADH) function:* Eggert, P., & Kuhn, B. (1995). Antidiuretic hormone regulation in patients with primary nocturnal enuresis. *Archives of Disease in Childhood, 73*(6), 508–511.

P. 95, *Seventy-five to 90 percent of children will stop wetting:* Geppert, T. V. (1953). Management of nocturnal enuresis by conditioned response. *Journal of the American Medical Association, 152,* 381–383.

P. 96, *Children are trained to hold their urine as long:* Edens, J. L., & Surwit, R. S. (1995). In support of behavioral treatment for day wetting in children. *Urology, 45*(6), 905–907.

P. 96, Dry bed training: Azrin, N. H., Sneed, T. J., & Foxx, R. M. (1974). Dry-bed training: Rapid elimination of childhood enuresis. *Behavior Research and Therapy, 12,* 147–156.

P. 97, Hypnosis *is an effective and long-lasting treatment:* Banerjee, S., Srivastav, A., & Bhupendra, M. P. (1993). Hypnosis and self-hypnosis in the management of nocturnal enuresis: A comparative study with imipramine therapy. *American Journal of Clinical Hypnosis, 36*(2), 113–119.

P. 98, Desmopressin (DDAVP): Thompson, S., & Rey, J. M. (1995). Functional enuresis: Is desmopressin the answer? *Journal of the American Academy of Child and Adolescent Psychiatry, 34*(3), 266–271.

P. 99, Imipramine *is an antidepressant:* Fritz, G. K., Rockney, R. M., & Yeung, A. S. (1994). Plasma levels and efficacy of imipramine treatment for enuresis. *Journal of the American Academy of Child and Adolescent Psychiatry, 33*(1), 60–64.

P. 100, *According to* DSM-IV, *soiling must occur once a month:* American Psychiatric Association. (1994). *Diagnostic and statistical manual of mental disorders* (4th ed.). Washington DC: Author, p. 107.

P. 100, *Encopresis occurs in about 1.5 percent:* Levine, M. D. (1982). Encopresis: Its potentiation, evaluation and alleviation. *Pediatric Clinics of North America, 29*(2), 315–330.

P. 101, *Once a child holds in feces, . . . events follows:* Levine, M. D. (1982). Encopresis: Its potentiation, evaluation, and alleviation. *Pediatric Clinics of North America, 29*(2), 315–330.

P. 109, *About half of all children with encopresis associated with constipation:* Loening-Baucke, V. (1996). Encopresis and soiling. *Pediatric Clinics of North America, 43*(1), 279–298.

5

DISORDERS OF ATTACHMENT

Richard J. Shaw and Anne L. Benham

VANESSA

Vanessa, eighteen months of age, was referred to our clinic by her social worker. She had been removed from her biological mother at age nine months and placed in a foster home, after being found alone in an abandoned apartment while her mother was high on cocaine. Her mother had used cocaine during the pregnancy and engaged in prostitution to pay for her drug use. After three months in the foster home, Vanessa's social worker was disturbed to find that Vanessa was eating poorly, not talking, and showed very little interest in exploring her world. Her foster mother confirmed that Vanessa appeared to be "lacking in vitality and unable to enjoy life." She was just as happy whether with people or alone in a room by herself. Her foster mother also acknowledged that with four other foster children, she was not able to spend the time necessary to encourage Vanessa to engage with her.

During her first few visits at our clinic, we made a number of important observations. First, Vanessa was extremely quiet and withdrawn, would not speak to anyone, and showed no interest in playing with any of the toys offered to her. Second, Vanessa had profound delays in her language and cognitive development, which we believed were a result of her serious neglect by her mother, compounded by the lack of individual attention in her foster home.

We recommended that Vanessa be taken out of her current foster home and placed in a new home with no other children, to allow her more individualized attention. Within a few weeks in the new foster home, Vanessa started to show some dramatic changes. She responded warmly to the attentive and encouraging efforts of her new foster mother to engage her in play. She started to smile and made her first attempts at speech. During a follow-up evaluation, we found Vanessa to be much more animated and social, and also clingy and distressed when her foster mother left the room briefly, indicating that she was starting to develop the emotional bond that we term attachment.

Vanessa demonstrates what we term a *disorder of attachment*. Deprived of the experience of a relationship with her own biological mother, Vanessa was then moved to a foster home where her foster mother had neither the time nor the energy to provide the nurturance necessary to help her overcome the neglect she experienced during her first nine months of life. Vanessa failed to develop an attachment to her foster mother, but as the experience in her second foster home shows, she did have the capacity to bond when placed in a suitable home. In this chapter, we describe what are termed the disorders of attachment.

Attachment is the term given to describe the bond that exists between the infant and his or her primary caretaker. Although it is well recognized that infants form attachments to different figures, which may include the father, one of the grandparents, or even a sibling, in most cases the primary attachment is with the mother. In this chapter, for the sake of simplicity, we refer to the mother as the primary attachment figure.

The infant shows attachment to the mother by smiling, crying, and calling out to her, to communicate states of hunger, anger, and pain. The infant seeks out the mother by crawling toward her and demonstrating a desire to stay close to her. The development of attachment appears to require both the presence of skin-to-skin contact between the infant and mother as well as the mother's ability to respond in an empathic manner by smiling, looking at, and talking to her infant. The primary responsibility for the mother is to create an atmosphere of warmth and trust, which facilitates attachment behavior. It is the nature of the interaction between mother and infant that determines the quality of the attachment relationship.

Attachment develops gradually, producing a feeling of security in the infant and a feeling of satisfaction in the mother. Healthy attachment leads to what has been referred to as a "secure base" for the infant, such that the infant comes to expect and rely on receiving support and emotional nurturance from the caregivers. It is believed that the infant's experiences over time lead to the development of what is called an internal working model of relationships. By this we mean that the infant's experiences with the mother during the first few years of life create a model for the infant that influences and determines what the infant comes to expect from relationships with other individuals. These working models may lead to patterns of behavior on the part of the infant as he or she anticipates future experiences in new relationships. Generally a responsive parent who is both empathic and supportive will foster the process by which the infant starts to explore the outside world, including relationships with other people. A mother who is able to create a consistent feeling of security and trust in her relationship with her infant is likely to promote the development of the infant's ability to form new relationships.

DEVELOPMENT OF ATTACHMENT

John Bowlby, a British psychoanalyst, known for his series of books on attachment and loss, first proposed a theory of attachment in which he describes the process by which an infant becomes attached to the mother. Bowlby believed that healthy attachment is essential for psychological development. Ethological observations led Bowlby to believe that attachment is a primary drive, whose evolutionary function was to ensure protection of the young. He saw a parallel for human attachment in the work of Konrad Lorenz, who described the phenomenon of *imprinting*, in which newly hatched young goslings appear programmed to follow the first animate object they see after birth. Further support for the importance of attachment came from the work of Harry Harlow, who studied rhesus monkeys raised in isolation from their mothers. He found that baby monkeys deprived of the opportunity to form attachments with their mothers grew up to be socially withdrawn, unable to reproduce, and, if impregnated artificially, unable to nurture their own offspring.

Table 5.1
Bowlby's Phases of Attachment

Phase I: Preattachment Phase (birth, to eight to twelve weeks)
- The infant has a poor ability to discriminate among individuals but can distinguish the mother's voice from that of other people. More recent research has also demonstrated that infants at this age show a preference for the smell of their mother's breast milk.
- The infant will orient toward the mother and track her movements visually.
- The infant has a preference for looking at faces and quickly starts to smile at people in the vicinity.

Phase II: Attachment-in-the-Making (eight to twelve weeks, up to six months)
- The infant becomes attached to one or more people in the environment.
- The infant starts to show social smiling and to respond to social cues with such behaviors as cooing and gurgling.
- The infant is able to recognize the parents and responds preferentially to them, but still does not express a consistent preference for one particular attachment figure.

Source: Adapted from Bowlby, J. (1969). *Attachment and loss: Vol. 1. Attachment.* New York: Basic Books, pp. 265–268.

The first three years of life are generally seen as being a crucial period during which infants develop their primary attachment relationships to the parents, and the experiences during this time set the stage for all future relationships. The stages of attachment are summarized in Table 5.1.

The growth of a secure attachment facilitates the process of the infant's being able to separate from the mother and then move on to explore and develop social relationships outside the family. Early research on children separated from or maltreated by their parents and on children raised in institutions with multiple caregivers has led to an interest in the question of attachment

Table 5.1 *(continued)*

Phase III: Clear-Cut Attachment (six months to three years)

- The infant shows the capacity for selective attachments, and will actively seek out and show a desire for contact with the primary attachment figure. This is the stage at which the infant is believed to be establishing a sense of a "safe haven" from which to explore the world.
- The infant cries and shows signs of distress when separated from the mother. The infant will also greet the mother and can be soothed when she returns.
- During this stage, it is common to observe the onset of stranger anxiety, usually around eight months of age. The infant starts to treat strangers with caution or withdrawal.
- This stage also marks the onset of separation anxiety around ten to eighteen months of age. The infant responds with distress when separated from the mother.

Phase IV (from three years)

- The infant sees the mother as a separate individual with whom he or she is able to develop an increasingly complex social relationship.
- The infant starts to engage in making plans to participate in attachment-related activities.

disorders in infancy and their long-term psychological consequences. Although the diagnosis of an attachment disorder is made based on behavior observations of the infant, it is implied that the disorder arises as a consequence of disturbances in the parent-infant relationship and that both the infant and the parent may contribute to these difficulties.

Classification of Attachment

Mary Ainsworth drew on the work of Bowlby to describe a classification of the types of attachment seen in infants. Using a paradigm called the *Strange Situation Procedure*, Ainsworth examined the response of infants ages twelve to eighteen months when they were separated briefly from their mothers, and their behavior following reunification. In the Strange Situation Procedure, the mother and her infant start in a playroom with a female observer. After a few minutes of play, the mother quietly gets up and leaves the room, leaving a purse or handbag as a signal that she plans to return. The behavior of the infant is observed both as the mother leaves and when she comes back into the room. At a later point, the infant is briefly left alone in the room. Ainsworth used the results of these observations to describe three categories of attachment, which have been widely adopted in research on attachment and are described in Table 5.2. A fourth category was added at a later date for infants who were not well described in the original classification.

DISORDERS OF ATTACHMENT

A secure pattern of attachment is associated with several indicators of good outcome, which include higher self-esteem, sociability, and general competence; infants with an insecure attachment pattern are more at risk for later emotional and behavioral problems. There has been considerable interest in the factors that influence the nature of the attachment in the infant.

Table 5.2
Ainsworth's Classification of Attachment

Secure Attachment
- The infant feels comfortable in the presence of the mother and is able to play and explore the playroom.
- The infant shows appropriate but not undue distress when the mother exits the room, leaving her infant with the observer.
- The infant seeks out the mother to be comforted when she returns to the playroom.

Insecure-Resistant Attachment
- The infant becomes extremely distressed when the mother leaves the playroom, and cannot be comforted by the observer.
- When the mother returns, the infant continues to protest angrily, alternately seeking out but then rejecting the attempts of the mother to comfort her infant.

Insecure-Avoidant Attachment
- The infant seems to be relatively unaffected when the mother leaves the playroom.
- When the mother returns, the infant appears either to ignore or actively avoid her. The infant nonetheless shows a high level of physiological arousal during the separation and reunion, suggesting a marked internal psychological reaction to the separation.

Disorganized-Disoriented Attachment.
- The infant shows fearful, confused, or conflicted behavior in the presence of the mother, indicating a disturbed and unpredictable relationship.
- This category of attachment is more prevalent in so-called high-risk infants and may be seen with abusive or substance-abusing mothers.

Source: Adapted from Ainsworth, M. D., Bell, S. M., & Stayton, D. J. (1971). Individual differences in strange-situation behavior of one-year-olds. In H. R. Schaffer (Ed.), *The origins of human social relations.* Orlando: Academic Press.

Studies of infants placed in residential centers where they do not have the opportunity to form exclusive relationships with primary attachment figures have shown that these children are likely to be more clingy and inappropriately friendly with strangers. Infants with parents who are stressed, irritable, depressed, or less attentive to the cues of their infants are also more likely to demonstrate an insecure pattern of attachment. Similar findings occur in families where there are high levels of marital conflict.

Reactions to Hospitalization

Infants and preschool-age children, even those with secure attachment to their parents, are particularly vulnerable to disturbances in their behavior when they are hospitalized for acute medical conditions, as demonstrated in the following case example.

LUCY

Lucy, a four-year-old girl, was brought to her pediatrician by her mother, who was concerned about a general decline in Lucy's energy level. A blood test suggested a diagnosis of leukemia. Lucy was referred to our hospital, which specializes in the treatment of childhood cancer. The diagnosis was confirmed following a bone marrow biopsy, and recommendations were made for an aggressive course of treatment with chemotherapy. Lucy's mother, who had three other young children and a husband whose job involved regular travel around the country, decided that she would not be able to stay at the hospital with her daughter. This decision was also influenced by her shock at Lucy's diagnosis and her difficulties facing the fact that her daughter had a potentially fatal illness.

The nursing staff were quick to observe changes in Lucy's behavior in the hospital. She became withdrawn and apathetic, avoiding eye contact with the staff and refusing to play with the recreational therapist. At night, she cried uncontrollably. Although Lucy's parents visited every few days, they were overwhelmed by the changes in Lucy's physical appearance. They sat next to her but were hesitant to touch her, and they seemed to have lost the ability to comfort her. During the first few visits, Lucy cried hysterically when her parents left, but after a week or so, she showed little reaction to their visits and at times seemed to avoid them.

We were consulted to evaluate the family, due to ongoing concerns on the part of the staff. What emerged in our meetings with Lucy's parents was that both parents felt extremely guilty for not bringing Lucy in earlier for treatment. They were feeling guilty for not taking more seriously the fact that she had been unwell for a number of weeks before finally consulting her pediatrician. In addition, they felt torn between the responsibility to look after their three other children at home, who were acting out more since Lucy's illness.

Clarification of these issues led to the parents' being able to come to terms with Lucy's condition, as well as appreciate the need for them to put their own feelings aside and provide more support for their daughter. They made arrangements to spend alternate nights with Lucy. Although nauseated and distressed by the side effects of the chemotherapy, Lucy quickly responded to the increased attention from her parents. She became more animated and, at the same time, more clingy, which indicated that she again felt connected with her parents and was able to turn to them for support and successfully complete her treatment.

Lucy demonstrates the characteristic sequence of behaviors that John Bowlby first described in his observations of hospitalized infants, at a time when it was not common for parents to stay in the hospital with their ill children. Bowlby described an initial stage of *protest* when the child is first left by the parents, in a scenario similar to that which we described earlier in Ainsworth's Strange Situation Procedure. Bowlby noticed how children cried inconsolably when first left in the hospital by their parents. He described regressed behaviors, including bed wetting and excessive clinginess. During the phase of *despair*, which follows after a few days, he noted that children can become aggressive, while at the same time appearing apathetic and withdrawn. During the phase of *detachment*, children resume their interest in play and interact more with the hospital staff, but paradoxically show less interest when their parents visit. After returning home, they may ignore their parents completely, showing evidence of anger and hostility, but at the same time they become excessively anxious if left alone by their parents. Bowlby believed that being separated from their parents during the hospitalization makes children sensitive to subsequent feelings of abandonment.

Generally these disturbances are short-lived, although the consequences may be more noticeable in children with severe and chronic medical illnesses that necessitate repeated hospitalizations. This research has led to a significant change in policies regarding hospitalization and a recognition of the importance of providing rooming facilities for parents when their children require hospital treatment.

Children Raised in Institutions

Children raised in institutions where they have no primary caregiver but are tended to by a rotating cadre of staff tend to have somewhat different patterns of behavior compared with those raised in the traditional family setting. These children may show a tendency to being withdrawn and apathetic. They interact little with their peers, and they generally seem listless and depressed. Others, by contrast, are inappropriately friendly with strangers and may appear to develop attachments with any interested adult figure. They often show an indiscriminate pattern of affection toward whoever happens to be available at the time. By the age of four or five years, these children have noticeable difficulties in their social and peer relationships. Temper tantrums are common, as are problems with concentration. As these children enter adolescence, difficulties in peer relationships and tendencies to aggressive behavior and poor impulse control are more common. These children are often quite demanding of attention in all of their relationships, and they become angry and hostile if they perceive that their needs are not being responded to.

CLINICAL FEATURES AND CLASSIFICATION OF DISORDERS OF ATTACHMENT

There have been multiple systems of classification of disorders of attachment. Reactive Attachment Disorder is defined in the *DSM-IV* classification system as a disturbance in social relatedness in an infant or young child, which leads to either failure to initiate and develop appropriate social relationships, or the opposite, a pattern of somewhat indiscriminate and overly social behavior, without evidence of genuine attachment to any particular individual. It is believed to arise from disturbances in the attachment relationship, usually the mother, who is presumed to help generate the disorder due to her inconsistent or neglectful behavior toward her infant. Disorders of attachment may be associated with signs of physical malnourishment and delays in social, language, and physical development. In cases where the height and weight of the infant are significantly less than expected for the infant's age, the term *failure to thrive* may be used. Failure to thrive is a general term describing a spectrum of disorders in which there is evidence of both malnutrition and developmental delays. Generally, both organic and nonorganic factors contribute to this syndrome. Some studies have shown a particularly high proportion of children who have an insecure pattern of attachment. Diagnostic criteria are listed in Table 5.3.

Recent work by Lieberman and Pawl, and Zeanah, Mammen, and Lieberman has led to a proposal of elaborating the number of disorders of attachment to five categories, to describe more fully the varieties of presentations seen in clinical practice. These descriptions, which we have found to be particularly helpful, are outlined in Table 5.4.

Table 5.3
Diagnostic Criteria for Reactive Attachment
Disorder of Infancy or Early Childhood

A. Markedly disturbed and developmentally inappropriate social relatedness in most contexts, beginning before age 5 years, as evidenced by either (1) or (2):

   (1) persistent failure to initiate or respond in a developmentally appropriate fashion to most social interactions, as manifested by excessively inhibited, hypervigilant, or highly ambivalent and contradictory responses (for example, the child may respond to caregivers with a mixture of approach, avoidance, and resistance to comforting, or may exhibit frozen watchfulness)

   (2) diffuse attachments as manifested by indiscriminate sociability with marked inability to exhibit appropriate selective attachments (for example, excessive familiarity with relative strangers or lack of selectivity in choice of attachment figures)

B. The disturbance in criterion A is not accounted for solely by developmental delay (as in mental retardation) and does not meet criteria for a pervasive developmental disorder.

C. Pathogenic care as evidenced by at least one of the following:

   (1) persistent disregard of the child's basic emotional needs for comfort, stimulation and affection

   (2) persistent disregard of the child's basic physical needs

   (3) repeated changes of primary caregiver that prevent formation of stable attachments (for example, frequent changes in foster care)

D. There is a presumption that the care in criterion C is responsible for the disturbed behavior in A (for example, the disturbances in criterion A began following the pathogenic care in criterion C).

Specify type:

   Inhibited Type: if criterion A1 predominates in the clinical presentation

   Disinhibited Type: if criterion A2 predominates in the clinical presentation

---

Source: American Psychiatric Association. (1994). *Diagnostic and statistical manual of mental disorders* (4th ed.). Washington DC: Author, p. 118. Reprinted with permission.

Table 5.4
Classification of Disorders of Attachment

I. *Nonattached Attachment Disorder*

- These children have not had the opportunity to develop a unique attachment relationship, and therefore they fail to demonstrate an attachment to any one figure, even when distressed or threatened. They frequently appear to be detached and removed, showing little interest in strangers.

- These children fail to show typical signs of distress or separation anxiety when separated from the primary attachment figure.

- This category of attachment disorder is common in children who have had multiple caretakers, children raised in institutions, or those with a history of neglect. It is not that they are unable to develop attachment relationships, but rather that they have insufficient experiences to allow these relationships to develop.

II. *Indiscriminate Attachment Disorder*

- These children show an indiscriminate attachment and will turn to any available adult when they are distressed and in need of comfort. If the child does have a primary attachment figure, it is notable that he or she will not automatically turn to this person when threatened or anxious. This characteristic has led to these children sometimes being labeled as "socially promiscuous."

- This category of attachment disorder is common in children who have a history of multiple foster home placements or in children raised in institutions.

III. *Inhibited Attachment Disorder*

- These children are unwilling to leave their primary attachment figure and often appear shy and withdrawn. They do not explore their environment in an age-appropriate manner. They may be described as clingy and dependent, and they are anxious in the company of strangers.

- A subgroup of children in this category of attachment disorder may be excessively compliant and anxious when they are observed in the company of their primary caretakers. In these circumstances, it is frequently observed that the children have been reared in an excessively strict and abusive atmosphere, and their compliance appears to be motivated by the desire to avoid upsetting the caretaker and incurring further punishment or abuse.

(continued)

Table 5.4 *(continued)*

IV. *Aggressive Attachment Disorder*

- The attachment relationships in children with this category of attachment disorder have a quality of anger and frustration, with aggressive feelings directed toward both the caretaker and themselves. They may express feelings of resentment and anger toward the caretaker following even minor frustrations, or manifest self-destructive behavior, such as head banging or scratching.

- This pattern of attachment disorder is more common in children raised in families where they either experience or witness physical violence.

V. *Role-Reversed Attachment Disorder*

- Evidence for this category of attachment disorder is seen in the behavior of children who are separated from their caregivers and show a characteristic type of behavior when they are reunited. Children may be excessively attentive and solicitous or, by contrast, punishing and rejecting. The overall quality of the parent-child relationship may be characterized by the child's taking on some of the role in caretaking that would more appropriately be taken by the parent.

Source: Zeanah, C. H., Jr., Mammen, O. K., & Lieberman, A. F. (1993). Disorders of attachment. In C. H. Zeanah, Jr. (Ed.), *Handbook of Infant Mental Health* (p. 339). New York: Guilford. Reprinted with permission.

ETIOLOGY

We have found that one helpful approach to understanding the etiology of disorders of attachment is to look at the characteristics of the parent, the contribution of the infant, the quality of the parent-child relationship, and finally external factors such as traumatic experiences, losses, or physical and sexual abuse.

Maternal Characteristics

There has been much interest in the mothers of infants diagnosed with disorders of attachment. It is common to observe mothers who report feelings of low self-esteem, inadequacy with respect to their parenting abilities, and poor coping skills. In some cases, the mother is depressed, as in postpartum depression, or suffering from a severe psychiatric disorder, such as schizophrenia. This is illustrated in the following case example.

SHEILA

Sheila, thirty-five years old, worked as an advertising executive in a busy New York advertising agency. She was a creative and energetic woman, with a flair for her work and an ambition to develop her career. The decision to have a baby with her husband, Paul, came only after considerable soul searching, reflecting her ambivalence about what this would mean for her professional development. Her own mother, who had a history of manic depression, had dropped out of college during her first pregnancy and never resumed her plans to go to medical school. Sheila had always determined that she would never repeat her mother's "mistake."

Sheila had an extraordinarily complicated pregnancy, spending much of the time on bed rest, before delivering a premature girl, Alice, who spent several weeks in the neonatal intensive care unit. Sheila, ambivalent about the pregnancy at best, went into a profound postpartum depression, leading to a two-week psychiatric hospitalization after she had expressed thoughts of wanting to suffocate her daughter. Her response to treatment was slow, and during this time, she was barely able to attend to Alice's needs. Her husband, Paul, enthusiastic about the pregnancy at the outset, was horrified at the prospect of having a child who might be vulnerable to developmental delays, which are common in premature infants; he withdrew into his work and was unable to provide support for either his wife or his newborn infant.

Alice, starved of emotional support from either of her parents, had difficulties feeding, and presented as a sad and withdrawn infant who showed little interest in the world around her. Her irritability and fussiness contributed to a vicious circle of neglect and emotional deprivation and a failure to bond with either of her parents.

Alice shows the classic features of an infant with a disorder of attachment due to emotional neglect. In other cases, parents may be overwhelmed as a result of their social or financial situation. Mothers who have children with disorders of attachment also tend to have higher rates of suicide, diagnoses of personality disorder, and histories of alcohol or substance abuse.

Infant Characteristics

It is always important to consider the possible contribution of the infant to disorders of attachment. One such factor is the presence of developmental delays or medical problems that interfere with the child's ability to bond with the mother. Many of these infants are described as having a difficult temperament with irregular patterns of feeding or sleeping, irritability, and problems with being soothed. These characteristics may have an important effect on the nature of the mother-infant relationship, particularly if there is not a good match between the temperament of the infant and the mother.

Mother-Infant Relationship Characteristics

Numerous studies have suggested a relation between disorders of attachment and the quality of the mother-infant relationship. The mothers of these infants are less likely to praise or show approval for their infants. They make little eye contact and do not seem to enjoy their infants socially. These mothers may not be well attuned to their infants' cues, responding in an unpredictable or confusing manner. For example, we sometimes see mothers who misinterpret their infant's cry for attention as a signal that the baby is hungry, and they attempt to feed the baby instead of providing physical comfort. In more extreme cases, the mother may be neglectful or critical or interact with the infant in an intrusive and overstimulating manner, all of which interfere with the attachment process.

Environmental Characteristics

Disorders of attachment are also likely to develop in infants who have had frequent separations from their parents, for example, children with serious medical illnesses that lead to repeated hospitalizations. Children are also at risk when there is a question of physical and sexual abuse, or abandonment.

DIFFERENTIAL DIAGNOSIS

The following disorders should be considered as part of the differential diagnosis

Pervasive Developmental Disorder

Children with Pervasive Developmental Disorder (PDD) have profound impairments in the quality of their social relationships, but they are usually alert and physically active, with no impairments in their nutritional status or physical development. It is less likely to find evidence of psychopathology in the parents of children with PDD as compared to families with disorders of attachment.

Mental Retardation

Children with mental retardation have global delays in all areas of their development, but their social and interpersonal skills are appropriate when adjusted for the child's developmental age. By contrast, children with disorders of attachment may have normal cognition and language but severe impairments in their social relationships. In addition, children with mental retardation do not show evidence of poor nutrition, although there may be delays in their motor development. There is no evidence of problems in the parents' ability to provide appropriate care, except in circumstances where the parents have symptoms of depression and withdrawal.

TREATMENT

Whenever there is suspicion of neglect, we recommend prompt intervention to ensure the safety of the infant. This may mean the decision to remove the infant from the family temporarily for a period of observation and assessment. Wherever possible, however, we recommend attempting to keep the infant with the parents, provided they have the resources and motivation for treatment.

Infant-Parent Psychotherapy

Infant-parent psychotherapy is a specialized form of treatment that we recommend for disorders of attachment, particularly with children younger than three years of age. Typically the therapy consists of meetings with the infant and one or both parents, all present in the same room. This treatment modality was pioneered by Selma Fraiberg, a social worker, and has been elaborated by Jeree Pawl, Alicia Lieberman, and others.

We use this mode of treatment for problems within the infant-parent relationship, recognizing that both the infant and the parent contribute to the problem, and in this way we try to avoid placing exclusive blame with either partner. We also recognize that children exposed to drugs or alcohol during the pregnancy and children with various developmental disorders raise particular difficulties for their parents. In these cases, being a competent parent may not be sufficient, and parents may need to draw on different resources and strategies to promote the healthy development of their child.

In some cases we may find that the past experiences and personality of the parents inhibit or interfere with their ability to provide the emotional support that their children require to develop a secure attachment, as shown in the following case example.

JENNIFER

Jennifer, age three years, was referred to our clinic by her pediatric endocrinologist, who was treating her for congenital hypothyroidism. Her mother, Margaret, age thirty-two years, a single parent, had two other daughters, ages seven and nine years, and although on welfare, she had worked previously as a dental assistant. She reported that Jennifer had recently killed one of the family's baby chickens, by holding its head underwater and then breaking its neck. Her endocrinologist was certain that neither her medical problem nor treatment with replacement thyroid hormone was responsible for this unusually aggressive behavior.

In our initial history, we heard that Jennifer had become increasingly aggressive at age six months, after her biological father was incarcerated on charges of sexually molesting Jennifer's two elder sisters. In addition to killing the chicken, Jennifer had tried repeatedly to strangle two pet cats and had bitten the ears of their dog. Recently she had started charging into her mother and sisters, and she had bitten one of her sisters on the face. Margaret reported that she had been unable to control Jennifer's behavior, despite having some knowledge of the principles of using time-out and other behavior modification strategies.

Jennifer was a vivacious and active girl who seemed to be well bonded with her mother. Margaret seemed comfortable interacting with Jennifer, although at one point during our observation, Jennifer violently twisted her mother's arm, to which she responded by just withdrawing her hand and then patting Jennifer on the head.

This unusual case raised some very interesting questions for us. Aggressive behavior in a young child often raises the suspicion of sexual or physical abuse, but despite careful questioning, we were not able to find any evidence of this. We were most impressed by the fact that Margaret was unable to set any limits on Jennifer's aggression, and in one incident, she appeared to reinforce the behavior by patting her on the head in an affectionate manner. Our preliminary assessment, however, was that Jennifer had the typical features of what we described earlier as an Aggressive Attachment Disorder. We recommended that Margaret and Jennifer be seen together in infant-parent psychotherapy.

During the treatment, Margaret gave us some additional history, which helped to shed some light on her inability to contain Jennifer's behavior. Margaret's firstborn child, also a daughter, had been "shaken to death" by a babysitter when she was ten months of age. This history, which Margaret had never discussed before, had led to profound feelings of guilt. Margaret believed that she had been indirectly responsible for this horrible tragedy, not only because she had returned to work early after the birth but also because she had selected the babysitter. Margaret had become severely depressed after her infant's death and was still troubled by horrifying nightmares about what she described tearfully as the "murder." In addition, in the years following this incident. Margaret described an abusive relationship with her husband, who repeatedly and sadistically assaulted her, often in front of their children.

At this point in this case, we were able to formulate several observations and hypotheses. First, Margaret was a victim of severe abuse, both at the hands of her ex-husband and more recently at those of her young daughter, and we thought it likely that we would find a history of abuse originating from her early childhood experiences. Second, there was an interesting parallel between the "murder" of Margaret's first child and Jennifer's cruelty to animals, including the killing of the chicken. Margaret's inability to prevent Jennifer's abusive behavior paralleled her inability to prevent the abuse of both herself and her children at the hands of her ex-husband. We often use the term *repetition compulsion* to describe the phenomenon in which a person seems compelled to repeat prior traumatic experiences, and we believed that Margaret was caught in a particularly vicious reenactment. This hypothesis was confirmed as the psychotherapy progressed.

As Margaret worked with us, she described her early childhood with great emotion and feelings of sadness. She and her sisters were raised in a family where violence was routine. Her own father, an alcoholic, would come home intoxicated and beat their mother. During one session, Jennifer started to play in a particularly aggressive manner, ripping a leg from one of the dolls in the playroom. As Margaret tried to remove the doll, Jennifer turned on her mother and attempted to bite and scratch her. Margaret pulled away but was unable to control Jennifer's behavior. We intervened, firmly holding Jennifer to show that it was possible to contain a small child safely. We suggested that Margaret was having the same feelings of powerlessness as she had experienced both with her ex-husband and watching her father abuse her mother. In a cathartic moment, Margaret was able to connect for the first time her childhood helplessness with her inability to control Jennifer's aggression.

In individual meetings, Margaret went on to explore many aspects of her early childhood experiences, realizing for the first time that she had been sexually abused at the hands of her father. This helped us to understand how she had been unable to intervene to prevent the sexual abuse of her own daughters by her ex-husband. As she worked through these painful memories, including her grief and guilt at the loss of her first child, she found herself becoming increasingly empowered to control Jennifer's behavior both in the infant-parent sessions and at home.

This case gives a brief glimpse into the complexity of infant-parent therapy. The task of the therapist is simultaneously to attend to the manifest behavior and interaction of the parent and child during the sessions, as well as connect the psychological meaning of these interactions to the parent's past history. In Margaret's case, the feeling of childhood helplessness had left the mother powerless to contain the aggression of a three-year-old. The themes of abuse and the psychological need to reenact her earlier experiences could not have been addressed without the insights provided during the therapy.

In cases where psychotherapy is either impossible, as is increasingly the case with managed care, or unsuccessful, we may recommend either temporary or permanent out-of-home placement for the infant. Wherever possible, we recommend placing the child with a family relative, but in many cases, foster care is necessary. Our goal is usually reunification of the infant with the parent, and for this reason, we suggest regular visitation to maintain the infant-parent relationship. In other cases, however, the decision may be made to proceed with permanent removal of the child from the parent's custody, and adoption.

Disorders of attachment may present in many treatment settings: day-care centers, pediatric medical clinics, and preschools, to name just a few. It is important to look at the relational aspects of the behaviors. The "patient" in most cases is the *relationship* between the infant and the parent. Timely diagnosis and referral for treatment at this early age can prevent serious pathology in later life. Treatment provides an important opportunity for parents not only to improve the relationship with the child, but also a second chance to rework issues from their own childhood.

NOTES

P.115, *Healthy attachment . . . been referred to as a "secure base":* Ainsworth, M. D. S. (1967). *Infancy in Uganda: Infant care and the growth of love.* Baltimore: Johns Hopkins University Press.

P. 115, *It is believed that the infant's experiences . . . internal working model of relationships:* Zeanah, C. H., & Anders, T. F. (1987). Subjectivity in parent-infant relationships: A discussion of internal working models. *Infant Mental Health Journal, 8,* 237–250.

P. 115, *John Bowlby, a British psychoanalyst, known:* Bowlby, J. (1969). *Attachment and loss: Vol. 1. Attachment.* London: Hogarth Press; Bowlby, J. (1973). *Attachment and loss: Vol. 2. Separation, anxiety and anger.* London: Hogarth Press; Bowlby, J. (1980). *Attachment and loss: Vol. 3. Loss, sadness and depression.* New York: Basic Books.

P. 116, *He saw a parallel for human attachment in the work of Konrad Lorenz:* Lorenz, K. Z. (1981). *The foundations of ethology.* New York: Springer.

P. 116, *Further support for the importance of attachment came from the work of Harry Harlow:* Harlow, H. F. (1958). The nature of love. *American Psychologist, 13,* 673.

P. 118, *Ainsworth used the results of these observations:* Ainsworth, M. D., Bell, S. M., & Stayton, D. J. (1971). Individual differences in strange-situation behavior of one-year-olds. In H. R. Schaffer (Ed.), *The origins of human social relations.* London: Academic Press.

P. 121, *Lucy demonstrates the characteristic sequence:* Bowlby, J. (1969). *Attachment and loss: Vol. 1. Attachment.* London: Hogarth Press.

P. 123, *There have been multiple systems of classification:* American Psychiatric Association. (1994). *Diagnostic and statistical manual of mental disorders* (4th ed.). Washington, DC: Author; World Health Organization. (1992). *International classification of diseases: Clinical descriptions and diagnostic guidelines* (10th ed.). Geneva: Author; World Health Organization (WHO). (1992). *International classification of diseases: Clinical descriptions and diagnostic guidelines* (10th ed.). Geneva: Author.

P. 123, *Some studies have shown a particularly high proportion of children:* Valenzuela, M. (1990). Attachment in chronically underweight young children. *Child Development, 61,* 1984–1996.

P. 123, *Recent work by Lieberman and Pawl, and Zeanah, Mammen, and Liebermann:* Lieberman, A. F., & Pawl, J. H. (1988). Clinical applications of attachment theory. In J. Belsky & T. Nezworski (Eds.), *Clinical implications of attachment.* Hillsdale, NJ: Erlbaum; Lieberman, A. F., & Pawl, J. H. (1990). Disorders of attachment and secure base behavior in the second year of life: Conceptual issues and clinical intervention. In M. T. Greenberg, D. Cicchetti, & E. M. Cummings (Eds.), *Attachment in the preschool years.* Chicago: University of Chicago Press; Zeanah, C. H., Jr., Mammen, O. K., & Lieberman, A. F. (1993). Disorders of attachment. In C. H. Zeanah, Jr. (Ed.), *Handbook of infant mental health* (pp. 332–349). New York: Guildford.

P. 130, *This treatment modality was pioneered by Selma Fraiberg:* Fraiberg, S. (Ed.). (1980). *Clinical studies in infant mental health.* New York: Basic Books.

FOR FURTHER READING

Kaplan, H. I., Sadock, B. J., & Grebb, J. A. (1994). Other disorders of infancy, childhood, or adolescence: Reactive attachment disorder of infancy or early childhood. In *Kaplan and Sadock's synopsis of psychiatry: Behavioral sciences, clinical psychiatry* (7th ed.) (pp. 1109–1115). Baltimore: Williams and Wilkins.

Lieberman, A. F., & Pawl, J. H. (1993). Infant-parent psychotherapy. In C. H. Zeanah, Jr. (Ed.). *Handbook of Infant Mental Health* (pp. 427–442). New York: Guilford.

Zeanah, C., & Emde, R. N. (1994). Attachment disorders in infancy and childhood. In M. Rutter, E. Taylor, & L. Hersov (Eds.), *Child and adolescent psychiatry: Modern approaches* (3rd ed.) (pp. 490–504). Oxford: Blackwell Science.

Zeanah, C. H., Jr., Mammen, O. K., & Lieberman, A. F. (1993). Disorders of attachment. In C. H. Zeanah, Jr. (Ed.), *Handbook of infant mental health* (pp. 332–349). New York: Guilford.

CHAPTER

6

GENDER ISSUES

James Lock, Victor G. Carrion, and Brian N. Kleis

TIM

Tim, age five, was referred to our clinic for evaluation by his pediatrician. His parents were concerned because since the age of two, he had preferred to play with dolls, tea sets, and other stereotypical female-oriented toys. He engages in a fantasy play that includes designing dresses and hair styles and is not interested in playing with traditionally male toys. His parents describe him as soft-spoken, gentle, sensitive to the feelings of other children, and very close to his father, who has provided a great deal of his parenting needs.

Tim acknowledged that he does not like to be a boy, and when asked he says he would prefer to be a girl. His behavior and mannerisms are also more typically female in nature. He came to the office wearing a blue and pink shirt, which he insisted on calling a blouse. He also had a colorful bracelet made out of strings, which he enjoyed and wore gracefully. At bath time, he would tuck his penis between his legs to make it look as if he did not have one.

His parents thought this behavior would eventually subside, but they have been getting more complaints from school because he is being teased by other boys. They were worried that his behaviors have become more fixed and that eventually he will be gay. They

feel frustrated and scared and went to their pediatrician, who eventually referred them to us.

⌒

We are three child psychiatrists who work with children with
Gender Identity Disorder (GID). Two of us (Dr. Lock and Dr.
Carrion) work in an academic setting and see patients by referral
from the surrounding clinic. Dr. Kleis is in private practice
within a multidisciplinary group practice and sees patients in his
community-based office. All of us have worked with children in
inpatient, partial hospitalization, and outpatient settings.

In this chapter we discuss ways to think about and treat children with GID. Although this chapter could be placed in a book
about either preschoolers or school children, we opted for its
description here. Even though many of the behavioral sequelae
occur during the school years, the onset occurs earlier, and evaluations and treatment should begin then. Our approach to children with these problems may differ in some respects from that
of other clinics because we believe that the fundamental problems that children with GID experience are for the most part
due to reactions to them rather than inherent problems with
them. Their own behaviors occur naturally to them. Much like
some other child psychiatric problems, Oppositional-Defiant
Disorder, for instance, the child's problems are secondary. The
young boys and girls with GID do not feel bad or ashamed until
parents and peers make them so, or they are the focus of parental
conflict that enhances gender-atypical behavior by adding an
emotional valence to it.

Like Tim, most children with GID not only engage in cross-
gender activity through fantasy and actual play, but prefer this
to games or play assigned to their own gender. This exploration
may be accompanied by distress regarding their gender. Personality characteristics will usually also correspond to those
expected in the opposite gender. Parents are concerned with

their inability to change these behaviors and worry about the sexual orientation of their child. They and others are also concerned about the social problems that their child will experience if these behaviors do not change. These parental concerns are the usual reasons for referral.

In this chapter we review the developmental context of gender identity and GID, discuss the evaluation of a child with GID, and provide examples of ways to assist children and their families with GID.

GENDER DEVELOPMENT

We have found that many people are confused about the terms *sex identity* and *gender identity*, so it is important to define these terms at the outset. Sex identity is the biologic sex, gender identity is the self-identification of oneself as belonging to a gender, and gender roles are the behaviors associated with a particular sex within a culture or group. GID is concerned with each of these to a degree. It used to be believed that a child with gender role nonconformity always reflected dissatisfaction with his or her biological sex. However, many times these feelings may be a reaction to social disapproval of their gender nonconformity. Referral rates for GID are estimated to be six-to-one to thirty-to-one favoring boys. These figures may be indicative of the narrower role of acceptable gender-specific behaviors for males. There are no formal prevalence studies of GID. Most researchers and clinicians describe the condition as rare.

Normal Gender Development

We find it helpful in our evaluation of children with gender-atypical behaviors to review those behaviors in the context of usual development of sex and gender awareness and behaviors in early childhood.

Within the first to fourth month of life, infants of both sexes enjoy many of the sensations associated with nursing, diapering, and the cleansing of the genitals. Infant boys are more likely to discover the genitals earlier than girls. The movement from genital play and exploration to masturbation is a gradual one that extends into the second year of life. For the most part, the genital self-stimulation of girls is less frequent, occurs later, and is less focused than that of boys. In children of both sexes, the ability to provide self-stimulation and pleasure contributes to their feelings of autonomy, control, and mastery.

In the second year of life, there is an increase in genital orientation and awareness. Self-stimulation is more focused, intense, and frequent, and it is often accompanied by genital pride and exhibitionism. In the latter part of the second year, the child may begin to develop a primitive form of fantasy life associated with self-stimulation. This pattern is fairly well established and remains more or less constant. Girls may use indirect methods of self-stimulation (using their legs, thighs, or toys, for example).

As children grow, their erotic interests become more diverse and may include peers and siblings. Games such as mommy and daddy or doctor are common; by age four, half of American preschoolers are involved in sex games or masturbation. Children's concepts of sexuality at this stage are quite rudimentary: many believe that infants are born by cutting the mother's stomach open or exiting through the mother's anus. In this age period, parental concerns with gender and investment in gender behavior are an important part of a child's perception of how to behave along these lines. Both direct and subtle messages about self-worth are contained in these parental and familial messages. This may be a special concern for boys because emphasis on achievement, competition, and control of emotional expression are the norm for both parents when raising boys, as is intolerance of behaviors that deviate from a traditional male stereotype. In this regard at least, boys are less free to explore cross-gender behaviors in our culture than girls are. There is a strong parental belief that boys need to behave in a much narrower range of gender role behaviors than girls. Parents are more likely to predict atypical outcomes (such as homosexuality) in boys with feminine behaviors than in girls with masculine behaviors.

Studies of gender identification found that at twenty-four months of age, children were aware of gender labels, but most did not consistently categorize themselves correctly. At thirty months, they were better at such classification, but it was not until age thirty-six months that children were quite certain of both their own and another person's gender. A number of studies have demonstrated that gender constancy develops later than gender labeling. Gender constancy encompasses both gender stability and gender consistency. This understanding requires some of the cognitive processes associated with concrete operational thinking. Consistency as a separate element appears to require practice as well and develops even later.

Although there is some drop in sexual activity and apparent erotic interest in children at about age five, children continue to be concerned with sexuality. In Kinsey's 1953 study, 57 percent of males and 48 percent of females who were interviewed as adults remembered engaging in sexual play between the ages of eight and thirteen. Among males interviewed when they were prepubescent, 70 percent claimed they engaged in some sex play. After age seven, relationships tend to be with same-sex peers. On the playground, sexual topics are common, especially with boys. By this time, children are well aware of adult prohibitions around sex and endeavor not to be caught. Nevertheless, games of Truth or Dare or strip poker remain common.

Sexual exploration in early and middle childhood is common. School-age years are associated with group behavior and divide most clearly along gender lines. Boys and girls are asked to perform uniformly and narrowly in the lowest common denominator of gender behavior in order to find a place among their peers. Those who do not risk ostracism and ridicule. Again, this appears to be a special problem for boys. Paradoxically perhaps, studies indicate that boys' peer groups (ages nine to eleven) use their group activities for varying levels of sexual arousal, including using sexually oriented language, viewing erotic materials, and disparaging other males with sexually laden terms, usually with negative homosexual content. These boys are likely to be using the group to manage their own personal anxieties about their gender roles.

Theoretical Origins of GID

There are two major types of theories to account for the development of GID, though neither has substantial evidence to support it. The biologic theories use genetic and hormonal studies to argue for a biologic basis for GID, but supporting evidence is still very limited. Psychoanalytic theorists look to familial, especially parental, factors as the root cause of GID. They report that family studies of boys with GID show that fathers are absent in 34 to 85 percent of the families, and in those families with a father present, he notably spent less time interacting with the son with GID in early childhood. Mothers in these families are reportedly hostile toward males and view their husband as potentially violent and out of control. As a result, these mothers supposedly discourage rough-and-tumble play and are often harsh and authoritarian disciplinarians. Psychoanalytic perspectives also argue that boys with GID are anxious about maternal withdrawal and abandonment (over 60 percent meet criteria for Separation Anxiety Disorder) and identify with the mother as a strategy to assuage the anxieties associated with separation and loss.

Girls with GID are not clearly accounted for in these theories. In addition, the studies on which these conclusions are based are very limited in number and do not control for different parental interactions with a child as a result of their cross-gender behaviors. For example, a father's own emotional responses and sense of identity may promote a more distant relationship with a boy who exhibits traditionally female behaviors, so it is hard to tell which came first: the feminine behaviors or the father's distance.

Parents are concerned that their children with gender non-conformity in childhood will become homosexual. Homosexuality is not a disorder, but even enlightened parents worry about how their children will be treated if they are homosexual. Others, including some psychoanalysts and researchers in GID, are concerned that these children will later become transsexuals. Some assume that GID leads to adult transsexualism. However, some sources have documented that transsexualism occurs in less than 10 percent of children with gender nonconformity when followed up as adults.

In a study of existing longitudinal data, Kohlberg found little or no correlation between standard measures of childhood masculinity and femininity and heterosexuality in adulthood. However, some studies of adult homosexuals' childhood memories of atypical gender behaviors support data that some degree of gender nonconformity may predict later homosexuality. These studies have been criticized because it is likely that homosexual persons are more comfortable remembering such behaviors than heterosexuals are. A number of studies of boys referred for gender nonconformity have been found to grow up to be homosexuals at high rates, but these studies may represent a particular subset of homosexuals. In fact, most homosexual adults identify with their gender and operate successfully with their gender roles. Homosexual orientation does not necessarily influence gender conformity. However, societal intolerance about being homosexual may influence gender role experimentation during the process of identity formation.

DIAGNOSTIC ISSUES

According to *DSM-IV,* GID in children is characterized by a strong and persistent cross-gender identification manifested in at least four of the following areas: their fantasies, desires, play, dress, or playmate preference. There is also a persistent discomfort with the gender role of their sex.

The most important consideration in making an assessment of GID is distinguishing between predictable cross-gender exploration and play from gender-atypical behaviors, which are rooted in the child's persistent and intense distress about being of his or her biological sex. The quality of persistence is best assessed by several factors, including the age of the child, the length of time the behavior or belief has existed, and the determination with which the behavior is held onto in spite of social approbation. In general, the older the child is, the longer the gender-atypical behaviors have persisted, and the greater the resistance is to changing the behaviors, the more likely it is that the child has a true GID.

Evaluation

When you are presented with a case of GID, you must understand clearly what the issues and concerns are for the parents and for the child. In the case of Tim, for example, his distress may result from some issues that are different from what evokes distress in his parents. He may be upset because his parents interrupt his play with dolls and because he is not allowed to pretend he is a stewardess; his parents are concerned about what they feel is inappropriate behavior in a boy and about his future sexual orientation. Other concerns may be more commonly shared. For example, both Tim and his parents experience distress over his being teased at school. This common concern is a good place to start because it unifies the family on a common goal: avoiding getting teased. All concerns must be addressed, however, and each individual concern may be dealt with separately. Tim's parents may benefit from psychoeducation on the distinction between gender identity and sexual orientation; Tim may be more interested in knowing how he can incorporate his wishes and fantasies in his behaviors and play without being reprimanded for his choices.

We always take a thorough history, because there are other emotional problems associated with GID. We are especially concerned if there is any evidence of oppositionality, depression, or anxiety. We want to know if there were any specific events that preceded a sudden onset of gender-atypical behaviors. Factors such as familial stress, death of a parent, birth of a sibling, and other traumas may be associated with brief periods of gender-atypical behaviors. These adjustment factors should be considered in any assessment.

In addition a comprehensive evaluation should include a physical examination. For children with GID, it is extremely rare for there to be actual medical problems that account for their symptoms. Parents, however, often have concerns that there may be anatomical or hormonal problems that are causing GID. To date, evidence of this exists only for children with intersex disorders who may develop problems with their gender identity as a result of familial or personal ambivalence or confusion about their sex identity. Some examples of these rare disorders include Turner's Syndrome (a condition where a girl is missing a female chromosome so that she does not develop expected secondary female characteristics), Klinefelter's Syndrome (a condition where a boy has an extra female chromosome so that he does not develop some secondary male sex characteristics as expected), and Hermaphrodism (an extremely rare condition characterized by the presence of both male and female genitalia). In each of these disorders, the child's sexual development is not as expected, so concerns about GID may emerge.

Mental Status Examination

Although Tim could give us an account of his problems by his report, behaviors, and play, a full mental status exam of the child is required. Successful interviewing of children requires that you approach the patient with awareness of the developmental capacities of the child. Questions should be straightforward, direct, and posed without embarrassment. Correct terminology for all body parts should be used. For younger children, anatomically correct dolls may be employed as an aid. However, you should be knowledgeable in their proper use and understand their limitations. Available research suggests that information gathered from play with dolls is not a definite marker of trauma or distress in the absence of verbal accounts. Further, you must avoid suggestion by dress or appearance of the doll. Patience and support are also necessary, as children may require extra time and encouragement to answer these types of inquiries. It is not unusual for children, especially boys, to feel very uncomfortable about being questioned in these areas because they are already sensitized to them. We have found that it may take several interviews before they feel comfortable enough to disclose, even in play, their true feelings and wishes.

With younger children, initial interviews often take place with one or both parents present. In Tim's case, we noticed his closeness to his father. In other children, we may notice that the child is so involved in his fantasy world that he rarely interacts with his parents. We also assess how parents interact with each other, as this may reflect some of their cultural views on gender, as well as any marital problems that may complicate a child's symptomatic expression. Finally, we assess if the child's interaction and behaviors with the examiner are any different than they are with his parents. This may provide clues regarding the nature of the gender exploration. In other words, is it more related to emotional problems with the parents than true gender role distress?

The Family Interview

Evaluation of the child's family is paramount in order to understand the environment that the child experiences. The greater the mismatch there is between the behavior and the caretakers' disapproval, the greater the distress is that the child experiences, a situation that leads to further tension in the relationship between the child and caretaker. In fact, some theorists think that the emotional difficulties of children with GID arise from parental and social intolerance.

An evaluation of the family needs to look at the following points:

- *Gender roles in the family:* The gender roles exhibited by parents and siblings are those the child has been exposed to and that he may model. For example, the son of a male model may be more concerned about his hair and his looks than the average boy as a result of wanting to identify with his dad.

- *Parental relationships with their own parents and siblings:* Family dynamics need to be assessed in order to rule out any possibility that parental distress is less related to gender and more an issue of the child's behaving more like another significant figure in the parent's life. For example, a mother who complains about her daughter's being just like her maternal uncle may be upset because of her feelings toward her brother and not necessarily because the child's behaviors are dysfunctional in any way.

- *Cultural and racial implications:* Some cultures place less emphasis on assertiveness and competition than that placed by the Western tradition. Less rough-and-tumble play can be expected in males from other cultures.

- *Marital division of labor and responsibilities by gender:* This information may assist in understanding the family's expectations of the child's behavior.

- *Medical conditions:* Any medical problem that increases dependency and limits a child's ability to explore peer relations can add to the difficulty of assisting a child with atypical gender behaviors.

It is important for us to keep historical and cultural factors in mind when working on issues of sexual behavior. Today, especially in regions that are home to many different cultures, variations between and among cultures can increase children's confusion about how to understand sexuality and sexual behavior. Parental attitudes based in various cultural belief systems can be at odds with the prevailing peer group attitudes of their children, adding to the confusion. When we work with children with sexual problems, we need to be aware of cultural belief systems to facilitate solutions to evolving conflicts among family members in these areas.

Further evaluation of the family includes an assessment of their psychological mindedness and flexibility. Psychoeducation about this sensitive issue is necessary in order for parents to understand and carry out treatment recommendations. Finally, evaluate how parents use their authority and power in their system. Authority that is used to provide guidance and safety can lead to support and reassurance; however, increased parental frustration and individual dynamics may lead to abuse. It is important for you to be able to interview children sensitively in order to determine if the child has been sexually, physically, or emotionally abused or is at risk for such abuse.

Social Problems

Children with a GID are likely to develop significant problems with peer relations, especially as they age and depend more on peers for social interaction. Children in the school-age years are anxious about gender role behavior and are intolerant of variations from stereotypes. By the age of five or six, peers of the same sex begin to shun these children, and by age eight or nine, even children of the opposite sex stay away. Thus, children, especially boys with GID, are likely to be teased and harassed by their peers. The result may be school avoidance, truancy, and other behavior problems. The children are also likely to develop lower self-esteem, which is to some degree dependent on social approval. Separation anxiety is a common confounding condition for those with GID, and these difficulties add to the burden of both familial and peer interactions. This separation anxiety may be fueled by fear of rejection by others outside of family members. When present, Separation Anxiety Disorder, depression, or Oppositional Defiant Disorder should be treated in conjunction with the GID. One boy we treated, seven-year-old Tony, had some long-standing opposite-gender behaviors; he became increasingly preoccupied with these behaviors during a custody battle when he was threatened with the loss of his mother as his primary caregiver.

PSYCHOTHERAPEUTIC TREATMENTS

Treatment for GIDs is a conflict-ridden area in child and adolescent psychiatric practice. Some practitioners argue that children with gender nonconformity are being treated inappropriately because the problem is not their behavior so much as others' response to it. These practitioners believe that education of the parents and communities about the acceptability of these behaviors is preferable to teaching the child to hide or change what comes naturally to him or her. More conventional approaches try to assist these children in finding safe opportunities to play in whatever way they choose, assist parents in understanding the need to support and love their child, and help the children to understand the reactions of peers and others. Still others use varieties of psychoanalytic approaches, including working with concepts of enmeshment and overidentification with the mother figure and attempts to try to change core gender identity. No systematic data on the effectiveness of any of these treatments, whatever their explicit aims, are available.

Behavioral Approaches

Behavioral approaches to discourage gender-atypical behaviors employ the usual techniques for positive reinforcement of gender-stereotypic behaviors. Specific behaviors are targeted for change, and rewards are developed to encourage the changes. These approaches have not been systematically studied, but some improvements have been noted on specific behaviors. A technical problem with this approach is that specific behavioral treatments do not generalize to other cross-gender behaviors (for example, cessation of cross-dressing does not lead to decreased play with dolls).

Other Psychotherapies

The principal goal of psychotherapeutic treatment for GID is to reduce the child's anxiety and unhappiness. Often these problems are not associated with the gender-atypical behaviors themselves but with parental and social reactions to them. There are a variety of common problems that clinicians face when treating patients with GID. Resistance to change on the part of the family and the child is predictable. Embarrassment and shame, especially among fathers, is another common difficulty.

Work with group child-care settings and schools, when appropriate, should also be undertaken in order to protect and support the child. Occasionally countertransference problems can contribute to a therapist's inability to empathize and assist children and families with this disorder. Religious and moral beliefs about sex roles and homosexuality, whether in families or therapists, may confound treatment of these patients. We take a three-pronged approach to these issues and work with the parents, the child, and the school setting. We will describe our treatment of Tim as an example of our family treatment approach.

Our first task was to assist Tim's family with their own reactions to Tim's behavior. They were quite anxious about the behaviors and had tried to direct Tim toward stereotypical male behaviors. They had signed him up for a boys' soccer team and had purchased a variety of typical boys' toys. They also had actively discouraged his participation in cooking and cleaning and other stereotypical female activities, although his father routinely did all of these. The net result was to increase Tim's sense of being incompetent and feeling that something was wrong with him.

We recommended that the parents try a different strategy. Instead of focusing on the far end of the stereotypical activities, we encouraged them to identify gender-neutral activities that were acceptable and pleasurable for Tim—for example, plastic construction blocks, certain board games, and books with more gender-neutral character (animals and magical creatures). The goal was to promote a greater range of pleasurable activities for Tim, not to take away those that he enjoyed.

In addition, we asked the family to identify settings where conflicts around gender-atypical behavior occurred so that we could help to intervene to decrease these conflicts. One simple but important intervention with Tim occurred as a result.

Tim had a sister two years younger than him, and when he went shopping with his mother for clothes for her, a conflict always arose over Tim's wishes to try on and buy girls' clothing for himself. His mother would reluctantly agree in order to stop a public tantrum at the store. We advised the family to stop taking Tim with them on these shopping outings. In their place, Tim would be taken on another occasion to the boys' department to try on and pick out clothes that were acceptable to him. This simple strategy reduced considerable friction in the family and lessened the teasing at school because he was no longer wearing girls' clothes.

The parents were also encouraged to help Tim develop friendships with boys who preferred these gender-neutral activities, and this minimized the rejection by peers. We also encouraged his parents to help Tim find a safe alternative place to play (for example, in his room without parental criticism or with other boys who enjoy or do not object to his play). This helps to encourage exploration of other less gender-atypical activities in other public settings. We sought to promote the likelihood that Tim would find ways to relate to peers in more helpful ways, which might assist in maintaining an overall positive self-image. These interventions were designed to lower the conflict about gender-related topics by removing the pressure on Tim to perform in ways that were clearly uncomfortable for him.

In addition to these practical interventions, we spent time with Tim's parents discussing their feelings about gender. Although they were open to the idea of flexibility around gender roles and in fact had themselves practiced it in their adult lives through an egalitarian view of much work, including child care, their anxiety about the possibility of homosexuality was high.

In approaching this issue, we told Tim's parents that Tim might grow up to be gay, but that this would not be changed even if he changed his gender-atypical behavior because most homosexuals did not exhibit gender-atypical behavior in childhood. We also told them that homosexuality is not a disease and that it would be most helpful for them to consider this possibility like any other characteristic of a child they loved. Finally, we told them that although in the few studies we have of children with extreme forms of gender-atypical behavior a majority do become homosexual, a sizable percentage do not.

Helping the parents to understand their worries and assist them with their own potential rejection of their child requires a frank discussion of this sort. It is not easy and takes revisiting throughout the treatment process.

Play Therapy

Individual therapy for a child in the preschool-age group is most commonly structured in the context of play. Play for a child of this age resolves problems in much the same way as insight does in older patients. The goal of play therapy is to make it possible for the child to play effectively—that is, to be able to resolve issues and conflicts in play. One of the biggest problems children with GID face is the familial and social resistance to the structure of play that is effective for them. In this sense, we see it as our job to help establish a safe setting for effective play for children with GID.

JEFFREY

When Jeffrey started treatment, it was clear that he initially was ashamed and embarrassed by how he wanted to play. In other words, he only played at playing, a kind of "as if" playing that fit what he had by age eight learned was expected. He dutifully took out boys' toys and acted out a play scene, but without enthusiasm or pleasure.

This is the antithesis of play. Jeffrey had learned to be vigilant about exposing his gender-atypical behaviors, especially to strangers. We assist such children by helping them to develop more gender-ambiguous or -neutral play. We present toys, animal puppets, figurines, and play settings that do not automatically confer a gender direction to the play. In our verbalizations, we encourage the children to explore fantasies without the inhibitions that they have learned by supporting them when they take a risk. Let's return to Jeffrey for an example of this.

Early on in his play, Jeffrey had a boy character who said that sometimes he liked to play with girls' toys. The boy character that I (Kleis) was playing responded by saying that he even sometimes wished he could be a girl. To this remark, Jeffrey whispered confidentially, "So do I."

We have noted that as children become more comfortable in playing as they wish and less guarded, their internal tension drops, and pleasure returns to their activities. This increased comfort allows the child and the clinician to explore through the play the kinds of difficulties that the child is having and to resolve them in terms that make sense for a child with GID. One important aspect of individual treatment is to illustrate choices the child has. He can identify "safe" and "unsafe" places for him to engage in cross-gendered play. Unsafe places are the ones where he gets teased or admonished. He can engage in cross-gendered play in these situations if it is important to him, or he can choose gender-neutral play to avoid the teasing and save the cross-gendered play for a safe place.

In addition to providing a setting for safe and effective play, we also try to help children with GID identify ways to address the social problems they are experiencing with peers. We encourage them to explore using gender-neutral play in such settings if they see that as acceptable so they diminish the teasing and harassment from others. Helping children to see the advantages of improving their repertoire of play behaviors is a lot easier once you have established a safe setting for the gender-atypical play and a feeling of trust and acceptance. We approached this issue with Tim in the following way.

We identified that Tim enjoyed playing a variety of gender-neutral games and did not feel as if he was in any way injuring himself by playing such games with peers. He also recognized that peers did not accept all of his play and that he would have to find other ways to have that kind of play to avoid teasing. We encouraged him to play with his peers in these more gender-neutral games. This allowed Tim to compete and to win at times. This success improved his self-esteem without sacrificing his wish to play as he liked, and it greatly improved his peer relationships.

We have found that as children experience the gratification of social approval from peers, they become more willing to explore more gender-appropriate play. In turn, this has the effect of minimizing the risk for possible harassment from peers. In play therapy, the child can bring up any current peer issues, and the clinician can assist in providing the child with tools to manage peer confrontation.

School

In Tim's case we worked with his school through his parents.

We told his parents that there were likely boys in his class who were less stereotypical in their gender behaviors. We advised the parents to try to help Tim develop a friendship with another boy who, although he did not share in a majority of Tim's gender-atypical behaviors, could participate in it to a certain degree and tolerated it in Tim. This social success greatly enhanced Tim's feelings of acceptability with his peers, and his self-esteem improved in proportion to this. In addition, Tim's parents discussed their son's needs with his teachers, and with our support, they were able to communicate how they wanted Tim treated. They discussed a need to respect Tim for who he was and to protect him from undue harassment to the extent possible. These supportive measures helped to improve the overall social climate in which Tim lived.

Biological Treatments

The biologic theories of GID are based on genetic and hormonal studies that investigate sexual orientation. R. Pillard's study of monozygotic twins, dizygotic twins, and genetically unrelated adopted brothers found that 11 percent of the adoptive brothers, 22 percent of the dizygotic twins, and 52 percent of the monozygotic twins were concordant for homosexuality. More recent research is based on levels of prenatal hormones.

On the intersex conditions, independent of the genetic status as male or female, prenatal exposure to androgens seems to promote the development of attraction to females, whereas nonresponsiveness to androgens is associated with erotic attraction to males. To date, these treatments are not recommended for children who have GID with no other genetic or hormonal deficiency.

Children with GID do sometimes become depressed, and many suffer from Separation Anxiety Disorder. Although both of these disorders respond to medication, psychotherapy is usually the first line of treatment. For children with GID who experience these co-morbid disorders and who do not respond to more conservative approaches, the use of medications is warranted. There are, though, no specific medications to assist with GID itself.

MANAGED CARE ISSUES

Because GID is a rare disorder, most managed care organizations are unfamiliar with it and have few providers who feel qualified to treat children with these kinds of problems. This lack of expertise may cause some managed care organizations to be more likely to find and develop contracts with skilled providers. Unfortunately, it is also likely that some of these organizations will delay or deny needed treatments because of the limitations of their existing referral base. In our experience, it requires education of the reviewers for these organizations in order to get approval for a treatment plan. In Tim's case, the reviewer readily appreciated the initial need to help Tim, but we had difficulty sustaining the treatment over time because the problem was not considered "acute." We told the reviewer that Tim was likely to develop worsening depression and anxiety symptoms if his treatment were prematurely stopped. Ultimately we prevailed, and we were able to continue to treat Tim and his family.

PROGNOSIS

According to some studies, by the time GID children reach puberty and high school, approximately two-thirds of them are likely to have developed a homosexual orientation. A new set of social problems emerges because the sexual and aggressive impulses of peers are now near adult levels. Exposure to this now physically threatening level of harassment leads to significant risk factors of depression, truancy, and substance abuse. In families that are also intolerant of homosexuality, runaway behavior and homelessness are common. For children who do not become homosexual, harassment in response to continued gender-atypical behavior is likely to result, and these children face similar problems that homosexuals experience.

A very small percentage of those with GID may become transsexuals and determine to live their lives as members of the opposite biologic sex. Some of these individuals seek hormonal and surgical treatments to augment physically their psychological and behavioral cross-gender condition. The social, physiological, and psychological ramifications of undergoing sex reassignment surgery or hormonal treatment are beyond the scope of this chapter. We do not recommend exploration of this alternative until adulthood.

Helping children who do not conform to our cultural ideas about gender behavior requires that you embark on a considerable task of self-exploration. How do you feel about gender and gender roles? How would it feel if your idea of your gender was not accepted by others? If you were a child, how would it feel to be told how to play or to have fun? In addition to these questions, those of us who work with children with GID are faced with perhaps unexplored areas of homophobia and sexism that interfere with our ability to empathize and create an atmosphere of support and respect of a child and family who need help. Confrontation of all of these issues will help any therapist to grow and develop new skills that are applicable in all their therapeutic work.

The primary issue in helping children with a diagnosis of GID is to respect and support the developing child. Attempts to manipulate and control the behavior of such children out of prejudice and bias are not therapeutic activities. We hope that all clinicians who work with children with GID recognize the unique capacities of each child and use their skills to help them to flourish.

NOTES

P. 141, *In Kinsey's 1953 study:* Kinsey, P., et al. (1953).*Sexual behavior in the human female.* Philadelphia: Saunders.

P. 143, *In a study of existing longitudinal data, Kohlberg found:* Kohlberg, L. (1966). A cognitive-developmental analysis of children's sex-role concepts and attitudes. In E. E. Maccoby (Ed.), *The Development of sex differences.* Stanford, CA: Stanford University Press.

P. 143, *According to DSM-IV, GID in children:* American Psychiatric Association. (1994). *Diagnostic and statistical manual of mental disorders* (4th ed.). Washington, DC: Author.

P. 155, *R. Pillard's study of monozygotic twins:* Pillard, R. (1990). The Kinsey scale: Is it familial? In D. P. McWhirter, S. A. Sanders, & J. M. Reinisch (Eds.), *Homosexuality/heterosexuality: Concepts of sexual orientation.* New York: Oxford University Press.

P. 157, *by the time GID children reach puberty . . . approximately two-thirds of them:* Green, R. (1987). *The "sissy boy syndrome" and the development of homosexuality.* New Haven, CT: Yale University Press.

7

CHILD ABUSE

Mary J. Sanders and Scott R. Brown

Rock-a-bye baby on the tree top
When the wind blows, the cradle will rock
When the bough breaks, the cradle will fall
and down will come baby, cradle and all

CHILD'S LULLABY, AUTHOR UNKNOWN

The human infant is totally dependent on others for survival. This dependency may be both appealing and overwhelming at times for any parent. Parents who abuse or neglect their helpless infant or preschool child have become overwhelmed or allowed their needs to overshadow the needs of the child.

This chapter briefly presents etiological theoretical models from a developmental perspective to provide a framework for understanding how abusive behavior may occur. The subsequent effects of maltreatment on the developing child will be explored, as well as assessment, management, and treatment considerations.

VULNERABILITY OF THE INFANT AND PRESCHOOLER

"How could a parent do such a thing?" We ask such a question in response to stories in the news, such as Susan Smith's killing of her two preschool children by drowning. Recent novels such as *Goodbye, My Little Ones* and *Cradle to Grave* have also outlined the serial killing of children by their parents.

Most people have difficulty understanding why a parent abuses or neglects a very young child. Nevertheless, children from birth to age five are particularly vulnerable to abuse and neglect for a range of reasons. A central reason is that children in this age group are limited in their ability and readiness to report maltreatment. It is not just that they have insufficient cognitive and language skills to report maltreatment; they have not had sufficient experience in the world to understand that anything is wrong with the experiences that they suffer.

Vulnerability is tied not just to the capacity to make a report but to the physical fragility of the child and the range of functions that parents still serve for the child up to age five years. Thus, infants and toddlers are particularly susceptible to abuse in the forms of Shaken Baby Syndrome, a situation in which the baby suffers neurological damage or death as a result of being shaken. They are particularly susceptible to neglect in the forms of failure to thrive, diaper rash, skin burn, and lacerations due to lack of supervision and inappropriate expectations on the part of their parents and caregivers. They are particularly susceptible to Munchausen by proxy, a form of abuse in which the parent falsifies the child's symptoms such that the child is considered ill or impaired; the parents may be overwhelmed with their own needs and seek relief from the care of the child or the attention and approval of medical personnel, or both

The younger the child is, the less likely he or she is to display behavioral symptoms of maltreatment. It is hypothesized that toddlers and preschoolers do not show as many recognizable patterns of maladaptive behavior because they, being younger, have not suffered abuse or neglect for as long. When children do show signs of maltreatment, their behavioral symptoms do not tend to be recognized because the symptoms may differ from those displayed by school-age children and adolescents, as well as adults. Hence, abuse and neglect in the early years may not be detected even by astute professionals. Therefore, the maltreatment may continue or escalate. The younger the child is, the higher is the risk for lethal maltreatment or pervasive effects.

In addition to the fact of dependency, certain characteristics of infants also make them particular targets for maltreatment. Indeed, premature and medically compromised, physically handicapped, and temperamentally difficult children have all been identified as particular targets for maltreatment.

Children of this age are also susceptible to maltreatment in the forms of sexual manipulation and exploitation and physical battery. Children who have experienced one form of maltreatment have also typically experienced multiple forms. It is important for us to understand the full scope of possible forms of maltreatment, including physical battery and neglect, sexual abuse, and psychological maltreatment.

ETIOLOGY AND THE CYCLE OF VIOLENCE

The etiology of abusive behavior is multidetermined and includes such factors as perpetrator characteristics, cultural contributions, and interactive aspects of the parent-child relationship. Jay Belsky contends that there is no one pathway to abuse, but rather that abuse occurs when stressors (such as, the demands of single parenthood) outweigh protective factors (such as, the parental instinct to keep the child from harm).

The study of etiology of abuse is important toward understanding how best to intervene preventively and actively in the abuse process. Maxfield and Widom found in a prospective study that children who had experienced abuse were significantly more likely to engage in violent behavior themselves as adults. Thus it may be that the effects of abuse are precursors of future violent behaviors. This cycle highlights the importance of recognizing the effects of abuse and intervening to ameliorate these effects, not only for the psychological well-being of the young child but also to interrupt a possible cycle of violence. Certainly the effect of abuse on the developing child places him or her at risk for problems in future relationships.

EFFECTS OF MALTREATMENT

It is our working hypothesis that the unifying factor between maltreated children and their maltreating parents or caregivers is an impaired child-parent relationship. In addition to general coerciveness in these relationships, maltreating parents have been observed to interact less frequently with their infants, toddlers, and preschoolers than the normative parent does. The interactions that do occur are characterized by less supportiveness and more negativity, both verbal and nonverbal. A parent-child interaction that we have commonly observed in our practice is described below as an example.

THE JONES FAMILY

Mr. and Ms. Jones enter the waiting room with their toddler, Sammy, and infant, Chris. They check in as Sammy explores the room, bouncing on the couches and pulling books off the shelf. They have not brought toys for the children to play with. The parents pick up magazines to look at as they wait. Finally, Sammy makes his behavior known to them by knocking over a plant in the waiting room. Mr. Jones grabs him roughly by the arm and shakes him, telling him to behave. The parents return to their magazines.

In this example, the parent did not interact directly with the child other than to police him when he had created a disturbance. In our work with maltreating parents, we frequently observe similar patterns of interaction.

The quality of relationships is critical to healthy development in the infancy period. Maltreated infants are less able to derive comfort and security from their caregivers, and as toddlers and preschoolers they are less able to explore their environments competently.

Attachment

Bowlby suggested that an infant's survival is ensured when he or she attains proximity to an attachment figure. Initially infants elicit proximity through signals. For example, they cry to attract caregivers when they are distressed, and they smile, cling, and vocalize to maintain proximity. The predictable outcome of an infant's attachment behavior is attaining the proximity of a trusted person and experiencing a sense of security.

Considerable evidence supports the idea that infant patterns of attachment are tied to the behavior of the caregivers. Infants usually display pleasure or joy when they interact with a caregiver who is sensitive and responsive to their signals. Similarly, they are easily reassured and comforted by the caregiver in the face of strange persons or objects, brief separations, and internal discomfort or pain. However, infants whose primary caregivers are either abusive (providing inappropriate care) or neglectful (providing inadequate care) tend to show evidence of anxious attachment by being avoidant or resistive to the parent.

Both abused and neglected infants, toddlers, and preschoolers have been found to be anxiously attached to their primary caregivers and to show the anxious-avoidant pattern in particular. This avoidance is viewed as a defense or adaptation to unresponsive or inappropriately responsive care. These children—infants, toddlers, and preschoolers—show such stress-induced behaviors as stereotyped reactions of huddling on the floor or rocking in a chair and soiling their pants. The upshot of this research is that maltreated children are at particular risk to represent the world, and their place in it, in a more negative, helpless, and either angry or passive fashion.

The Self System

Not surprisingly, a considerable body of research has linked patterns of attachment with mothers and fathers to the development of the toddler's and preschooler's sense of self. Research on the impact of maltreatment on the development of the self is scant. Schneider-Rosen and Cicchetti found that toddlers' recognition of the self-image and reactions to the self-image vary as a function of maltreatment status. Specifically, they had toddlers apply rouge to their faces and then observed their reactions to their mirrored reflections. Normative toddlers were more likely to show recognition of themselves and an increase in positive affect following application of rouge to their faces, whereas maltreated toddlers were more likely to fail to show recognition of themselves and manifest neutral or negative reactions to seeing themselves with rouge on their faces.

Preschooler Adaptation

Again, not surprisingly, research has shown a pronounced relationship between patterns of attachment and adaptation in the toddler and preschool years. For example, preschoolers with anxious attachment patterns have been reported to have dysfunctional relationships with peers in comparison to securely attached children. J. Lawrence Aber, Joseph Allen, Vicki Carlson, and Dante Cicchetti reported that preschoolers who suffered from multiple and overlapping forms of maltreatment had significantly impaired readiness to learn and explore in the company of unfamiliar adults. Maltreated preschoolers appear to subordinate their desire to learn to the need to establish proximity and contact with unfamiliar adults.

Maltreated children have also been found to have disturbed peer relationships. Abused children have been found to be more likely to react to their age-mates with aggressive or provocative responses in a variety of contexts, whereas neglected children are more likely to withdraw from social interactions as well as demonstrate active avoidance or resistance to bids by their peers. It appears that maltreated youngsters do not enter into the peer world with a readiness to engage in positive or adaptive ways, and they respond to their peers in such a way as to reduce the likelihood of further interactions or elaborated relationships.

In spite of the data on the impairments of readiness to learn and peer relationships, maltreated children may not typically show overt behavioral symptomatology during the preschool period of development. Aber, Allen, Carlson, and Cicchetti, for example, found that maltreated preschoolers did not show greater difficulties in interpersonal aggression, depression, social withdrawal, and somatic complaints than control preschoolers.

ASSESSMENT AND REPORTING OF ABUSE

The assessment of possible abuse of the infant or preschool child may be especially difficult due to the child's difficulty reporting the experience. The assessment should include evaluation of physical findings as well as the observation of behaviors. However, you may not see behavior symptoms indicating abuse, and you may observe behavior symptoms that you attribute to other problems, such as chaos in the family. In conducting our evaluations, we request a physical examination so as to assess any physical indicators, gather descriptions from others (such as parents and day-care workers) regarding the child's behaviors and any significant changes in behaviors, observe the child's play (usually over several sessions), and depending on the child's ability to give narratives, attempt to interview the child in a non-leading manner. Sometimes we may be unsure whether abuse has occurred. However, if the child is displaying behavior symptoms, we may find that therapy may be helpful to the family, whether abuse was discovered or not.

If we feel that we have a reasonable suspicion of abuse, we report it to Child Protective Services (CPS). In these cases, we have found that a specific, step-by-step procedure is quite helpful:

1. We advise the nonoffending parent or guardian of our concerns and discuss with this person his or her observations of physical or behavioral signs.

2. We contact the alleged perpetrator and invite him or her to share information relevant to the suspicions of maltreatment and join us in making a report to CPS. Although the accused parent is typically defensive and denies the allegation, we have found that the person is typically cooperative and will participate in conference calls or conjoint meetings.

3. We submit a follow-up report within thirty-six hours to reiterate our concerns and the evidence, information about the parties involved, and the reactions of those parties.

CASE MANAGEMENT: CPS INVOLVEMENT AND PARENT ACCESS

Typically children who present for evaluation or intervention have been or are the target of a CPS evaluation. Often, as a result of CPS evaluations, the child may no longer reside with both of the parents, or the perpetrating parent may have been removed. This situation makes inquiries about who has legal custody of the child, and therefore who has the right to seek evaluation or treatment of the child, of central importance. Once custody has been determined, exploration of the CPS plan for reunification and the access that the perpetrating parent(s) has to the victim child is essential for clinical planning.

It is not uncommon for infants and preschool children to be removed from the home and placed in either relatives homes or foster homes due to their particular vulnerability. On the other hand, it is quite typical for states to mandate either rapid reunification or early termination for children in this age group so as not to exacerbate problems in parent bonding and infant-toddler attachment.

Mental health professionals—psychologists; psychiatrists; licensed clinical social workers; and marriage, family, and child counselors—have a duty to report reasonable or credible suspicion of maltreatment. Too often we have observed that clinical professionals have assumed that because a child is involved in the CPS system or because prior reports have been made, additional reporting is not necessary. This is not true. If you find that further abuse has occurred and has not been reported, you are mandated to report this information.

MANAGED CARE

Many of our families have some court involvement, and many of the children have been removed from the home. As a result, the children tend to be covered by county funds for treatment. The parents, however, are frequently mandated to come to therapy and must provide their own funding, whether through insurance or out of pocket. If the families are covered by managed care companies, we have found that the companies accept the referral (usually made by the courts) to our treatment center, given our expertise in the evaluation and treatment of abuse. Consequently, we have not experienced a great deal of difficulty making a case for evaluation and treatment sessions.

Another source of funds for treatment comes from the Victim's Witness Program, funded through the state to provide medical and psychological treatment to victims of crime. In order to be eligible for these funds, the victim must press charges against the alleged perpetrator. The telephone number for this program is listed in the White Pages of the telephone book in most states.

PLAY PSYCHOTHERAPY

In our work with maltreated infants, toddlers, and preschoolers, we conceptualize treatment as constituting a set of overlapping phases and modalities. In general we initially rely on play psychotherapy. In the event that the child has been or is going to be reunited with the offending parent(s), we engage him or her in parent counseling during this initial phase as well. Then we shift from working with the toddler or preschooler and the parent(s) separately to working with them jointly in order to address relationship issues.

Because children in this age group do not typically have the language or cognitive skills to engage in verbal or talk psychotherapy, we have adopted play psychotherapy as our central mode of treatment. For children who have a history of normative parenting and no trauma, play is intrinsically enjoyable and is the natural mode of learning cognitive and social skills. Play is also a natural modality for mastering upsetting experiences and reactions because the child is able to take a direct and controlling role in recreating situations that were overwhelming.

Play allows the child to express feelings and display behaviors, or communicate his or her experience. We have observed that maltreated toddlers and preschoolers, in particular, express their unidentified and conflictual representations, fantasies, and feelings more readily and more accurately through action than verbalization. In these periods of development, play also permits the child to achieve distance from reality through symbolization to the degree that it is not so threatening that it can be portrayed.

With a trained professional, client-centered play therapy helps the toddler or preschooler with a history of maltreatment build a different and trusting relationship with someone who will listen to his or her needs and respond sensitively and responsively without the complications of the adult's projections and identifications. Skill-centered play therapy encourages the development of basic play skills and symbolic play skills, which are impaired in children who have suffered maltreatment.

Psychodynamic play therapy techniques assist the toddler or preschooler in working through conflicts related to the maltreatment, such as anxiety, guilt, anger, helplessness, the perception of the self as "bad" or "unworthy," and the perception of others as unavailable and ungratifying, hostile, and manipulative.

Treatment Contract

Before beginning the therapy, we enter into a treatment contract with the family so that all family members know what to expect. If we are required to provide progress reports to the courts, we discuss the specifics. Appropriate releases are obtained if the sessions are to be videotaped. Also, although the children are quite young, we explain the limits of confidentiality to all family members and any needs we would have to discuss the therapy with others.

Setting up the Environment

In order to allow or promote the young child to engage in play, the environment must be particularly safe on a number of levels. One level, of course, is physical. Play psychotherapy should be conducted in a room free of objects that could be damaged and that the child could readily use to hurt herself or the psychotherapist. We also promote safety on an interpersonal level. For the sake of the child's comfort, we have found it useful to discuss the purpose of the sessions with the child and our rules for behavior. We say something like: "This is a room where we can play together for awhile. We can use the toys however we want, but we cannot hurt anyone, and we have to listen to each other. If you have to go to the bathroom or get a drink, just let me know, and we can stop for a few minutes. When we are all done, we will clean up the toys together."

We also have found it helpful to invite the child to share what rules he thinks would be important to make the room as safe as possible. No matter how childproof the room, children typically point to objects in the room that should not be touched. Depending on the child's age and history, we have been told such things as "no touching privates," "you can't hurt my ears," "you can't hurt my bottom," "no breaking the glass," and "you can't leave me."

The toys set out should be developmentally appropriate. For the child who is continuing to teeth, be aware of any objects that could be swallowed or broken by mouthing. The toys we use the most are drawing materials (nontoxic, water-based markers, crayons, paper), play dough, a dollhouse with dolls of a range of sizes and roles, people and animal puppets, cars and trucks and emergency vehicles, blocks, and baby dolls with bottles, blankets, and cribs.

Depending on the history of maltreatment, specific toys should also be considered. For example, with children who have witnessed violence, we often include toy guns. Kitchen sets with pretend food and miniature pots and pans may be particularly relevant for children with a history of nonorganic failure to thrive, and a doctor's kit may be particularly relevant for children with a history of Munchausen by proxy. Specific toys serve to stimulate particular kinds of play by giving children permission to engage in fantasy around those themes. Yet it is also the case that imaginative or determined children will use whatever means necessary to simulate specific toys. For example, as we all know, the index finger and thumb can be used to simulate a toy gun.

Selected Issues in the Content of Play Psychotherapy

The content of play psychotherapy depends on the therapeutic orientation of the clinician or the intervention modality that the clinician chooses given the particular difficulties of a particular client. There are no clear data on whether play psychotherapy that is characteristically client centered, skill centered, or psychodynamic is more or less effective in the treatment of abused or neglected children. Certainly, instruction in one or all of the forms of these psychotherapies is beyond the scope of this chapter. In this section, therefore, our goals are restricted to the issue of the therapist-client relationship, a review of play themes of maltreated toddlers and preschoolers, working with children with limited verbal skills to express and transform their experience, and countertransference issues.

Because relationships are so salient and difficult to negotiate for toddlers and preschoolers who have experienced maltreatment, we have found it helpful for play psychotherapists to be attuned to relationship issues. Two different systems of describing relationships are useful: the Parental Acceptance Scoring System and the Dyadic Connection–Separation Scoring System.

The Dyadic Connection–Separation Scoring System highlights different modalities in which adults and two- to five-year-olds typically engage: being together, touching, and mutual engagement around an object or toy. Maltreated toddlers and preschoolers often become overwhelmed or disorganized in the context of shared emotion and require connection on either the level of just being together or mutual engagement. On the other hand, when children have attempted to engage us in seductive or hostile touching, we have attempted to shift them into connection that involves joint effort or attention around a task, while keeping a distance between our bodies and their bodies.

Phases of Play Psychotherapy

Play psychotherapy with maltreated toddlers and preschoolers typically requires eighteen months to two years to conduct. Work in any one phase of the treatment is particularly slow due to the dynamics of the maltreated child of this age. Thus, we recommend that appropriate assessment and diagnosis be conducted prior to establishing a contract for treatment with the referral party, for example, the nonoffending custodial parent or CPS. Establishing a therapeutic relationship and therapeutic alliance only to have the child withdrawn from treatment due to a change in foster parents or due to difficulties with the biological parents who have perpetrated the abuse can cause further damage to the attachment system, concept of self, and concept of others. Thus, we recommend against attempting to do short-term or problem-focused play psychotherapy for this population of clients.

Phase 1: Establishing a New or Different Relationship. Because toddlers and preschoolers who have been maltreated typically are hypervigilant, manipulative, resistant, or withdrawn, establishing a different and trusting relationship with the child is often quite difficult. We find that the children we work with are often provocative, that is, they "pull for" hostile and angry reactions on our part or they are so fearful of abandonment that they do not engage at all with us.

We do not interpret the meaning of play, rather, we respond to the child's needs and display tolerance. Often toddlers and preschoolers cannot tolerate our joining in whatever feelings they display or our collaborating in their attention and manipulation of stimuli. Thus, our stance is to ask, "What should I do? How should I play?" Such maneuvers suggest to the child that she can direct the play and the actions of the psychotherapist and that this adult is available to her.

It is particularly important at this phase for you to look for signs that the child needs understanding, approval, guidance, and control and to respond appropriately. We have found that using the Parental Acceptance Scoring System is particularly helpful.

The Parental Acceptance Scoring System highlights four different domains in which an adult may provide "acceptance" of the child's needs: approval, synchrony, guidance, and noncompliance. Understanding the types of cues that a toddler or preschoolers may give to signal these needs, and the range of ways that these needs can be met, is critical. For example, coping with issues of noncompliance in maltreated children is particularly common as these children struggle for a sense of control in relationships. Clinicians are presented with the opportunity to assist the child in the need for control in transitions from activity to activity, when setting limits on the child, or when attempting to modify a child's behavior or agenda. The Parental Acceptance Scoring System will help you to adjust the particular options and incentives that you provide to the child and thus who you are to the child in simple and concrete ways.

Phase 2: Drawing the Child into the Frame of Play. Maltreated toddlers and preschoolers are often either reluctant to engage in play or unable to engage in pretend or symbolic play due to the nature of their experiences with their parents or caretakers. Several techniques have been useful in overcoming this obstacle. One has been to use toys or materials that are simultaneously intrinsically interesting or pleasurable to the child and do not call for the child to be particularly creative. Such toys encourage the child to play but do not demand that the child structure the play. Thus, while using play dough, the child can manipulate the materials to produce a product. Dolls from popular cartoons with pieces to manipulate or stories to enact are also useful for this purpose.

When we observe toddlers and preschoolers who lack the skills to engage in pretend play, we model actions, label behaviors, and ask questions to stimulate symbolism. For example, if a child is seated at a table in our "kitchen" with spoons, bottles, plates, or bowls, we might use a doll to encourage him to pretend at self-related activities. If the child spontaneously picks up a bottle and simulates drinking, you might say, "Oh, you're drinking. Are you having juice or milk? I'm going to have some cereal," and you can pick up a spoon and the bowl and pretend to eat. Then you may offer "cereal" to the child. Mirroring the child's actions with different materials helps to extend the child's play from the simplest to more and more complex actions.

Once the child has shown a readiness and ability to engage in a range of symbolism that directly involves his own body, such as eating, grooming, or dressing, the next transition is toward single schemes wherein the child extends the symbolism beyond his own actions. Typically, this means that he includes others, such as a doll or you as actor or receiver of action, and it means pretending to act as other people or objects.

Helping the child to make these transitions often involves modeling. For example, in the kitchen scenario, you may state that the baby is hungry too and that the child is going to feed the baby, pour the milk and cereal in a bowl, and then spoon the food to the mouth of the baby. The baby, through you, may make eating sounds, such as smacking or burping.

The next transition is toward combinations of symbolic games. At this stage, you help the toddler or preschooler by including other possible recipients of actions, such as stuffed animals that are also hungry, or asking about related activities that may precede or follow the schemes that the child is already manifesting. For example, once the baby has eaten, you may suggest that the baby needs to be changed and invite the child to change the diaper of the baby; then the child may be invited to put the baby to bed.

The final transition is toward symbolic identification. In this stage, the child shows symbolic identification of one object with another (for example, using a stick for a spoon) and demonstrates symbolic identification with that of another person or object (for example, picking up the doll and saying, "baby"). You may facilitate this transition by asking whether the child can pretend that a block is a box of cereal or that a cup is a bottle of milk. Such negotiation between you and the child also helps the child to conceptualize that one thing can represent another, for example, that dolls represent people.

Phase 3: Portrayal of the Maltreatment. Now that the therapeutic relationship is intact, the young child begins to use the materials to play out his experience. Your task at this point is simply to encourage these communications or the telling of the story. Often you are invited to play along, but you must be careful to provide sufficient scaffolding or structure so that the play will not become overwhelming without leading the child. Also, you must be careful not to interpret these pretend scenarios as having actually occurred since they may not have occurred. The importance of the child's engaging in the pretend play is to be able to express his own fantasy or experience and develop mastery.

Phase 4: Constructing Different Solutions. Since the child may present pretend scenarios that depict elements of abuse, you can help the child formulate different outcomes. For example, if the preschooler creates a story of being sexually abused, you can help him by encouraging him to say, "It is not okay for you to touch me there." In doing this, you are teaching the child that adults can take responsibility for their actions and be respectful of the child's wishes. These different solutions may help the child continue to develop mastery of past abusive experiences.

Phase 5: Termination. Ending this therapy can an emotional time for both the child and the therapist. You may be the first person with whom the child has been able to build a trusting, consistent relationship. Hopefully during the therapy, you have also been able to help the child build other such relationships outside the therapy, with either the foster family or other family she will reside with in the future.

The termination should be well planned so the child is able to spend adequate time grieving the loss and planning for the future. We plan special activities to do in sessions as we get close to the end, including having a party with important people in the child's life as a ritual for closure.

FAMILY TREATMENT

Intervention with maltreating families must take each family's cultural context and specific needs into consideration. You may help the family obtain needed services, such as housing, clothing, or food stamps, or provide specific parenting instruction. The goal of the interventions is to meet the family where it has the need and begin to build a collaborative relationship.

Parenting Groups

Frequently parents are mandated to attend parenting groups, which are designed to provide the basics in parenting skills, such as discipline techniques and the teaching of appropriate developmental expectations. These groups also provide an opportunity for the parent to hear the experiences of other parents.

Family Play

Parents benefit greatly from being able to implement the parenting skills they have learned (from the parenting groups as well as in our sessions) in interactive sessions with their own children. We have heard from the parents we work with that the ability to try out a strategy in the playroom has been a good experience; they can see how their child responds, and they are able to receive feedback from the therapist. If the child does not respond in the expected or desired manner, the parent may feel that she or the child is "bad." The ability to try these strategies in the room allows the parent-therapist team to work on refining strategies that were not as successful as hoped, thus averting a sense of failure.

The family play technique combines play therapy and parent training to provide both modeling for the parent and an alternative experience to the abusive experience for the parent and child. The goals of the family play are to enter into a contract to discontinue abusive behaviors, assess the parent's style of parenting and the child's response to it, provide direct teaching and modeling of healthy parenting behaviors, and encourage parent-child interactions that feel positive to both parties and promote healthy relationships.

In addition to the play sessions, we set up weekly meetings with the parents. We use these sessions to build a collaborative relationship, encourage the parents to acknowledge and take responsibility for their abusive behaviors, discuss parenting issues and plan for interventions in the play sessions, and review the videotapes of previous play sessions to examine the interactions we are focusing on and assess progress.

Phases of Family Play

The phases of family play incorporate individual play psychotherapy with dyadic family play, as well as individual and couple sessions with the parents.

Phase 1: Establishing a Relationship with the Family. Of utmost importance in the building of a collaborative relationship with the parent is to work together to meet the parents' and therapist's mutual goal of improving the relationship between the parent and child. A parent who begins to feel safe and accepted in the therapy experience is able to be less defensive about parenting and more open to examining ways in which to improve parenting skills.

In our work with the parent, we pay attention to the times in which the parent is engaging well with the child and point this out. We ask whether the parent found the interaction to be reinforcing and whether it was a positive or negative experience. As we continue to gather these examples of the alternative story to the abusive behaviors, the parent appears to become more aware that we are working together to build the experiences that she would like to have with her child.

We also notice with the parent the times that the child is engaging in behaviors that are difficult for the parent and acknowledge the parent's experience of these behaviors. We ask the parent to describe his experience during these times. Here we are attempting to understand the parent's experience—how he may feel invited into abusive behaviors as a means of coping. In this way, the parent feels heard and understood.

Phase 2: Assessing the Parent-Child Interaction. We first conduct an assessment play session, observing how the parent plays with the child, disciplines the child, and otherwise interacts. Again we use the Parental Acceptance Scoring System as a means of evaluating the parenting domains of approval, synchrony, guidance, and noncompliance. We videotape these sessions and then meet with the parent to review and discuss her goals to improve her parenting skills. This phase provides the basis for building our play session interventions.

Phase 3: Planning Play Session Interventions. Following the play assessment, we take the following steps to plan specific interventions and discuss how we will conduct the upcoming play sessions:

1. *Define the Problem:* The parent and therapist agree that the overriding problem is abusive behavior and that it can no longer occur. Then they collaborate to define lesser problems that may have invited the abusive behavior in the past—for example, the child does not obey a request. Many times parents report that when this occurs, they feel the child is being disrespectful, that they are "bad parents," or that the child is "bad." Many times the parents say that the only time the child listens is when he is spanked or has a major privilege removed. As a result, there may be no consequences for the "disobeying behavior" because the parent feels helpless, thus giving the child the message that he does not need to obey, or an extreme consequence that does not fit the misbehavior. Over the course of the therapy, the parent experiences alternative means of dealing with these lesser problems.

2. *Set Goals:* Goals will be individually specific. For example, we worked with a father who wished to decrease his "yelling behavior" and still be able to have his child obey his directives. Another example is a mother who felt she had to make angry threats to her children when they did not obey her directives. These goals are discussed in individual meetings with the parent and worked on in the interactive sessions.

3. *Introduce Step-Outs:* At times during the play sessions, the parent or therapist may ask to step outside the room for a brief discussion. By having the discussion outside the room, you and the parent can work collaboratively without the child's observing the interaction. The child is informed of this plan prior to the sessions and asked how it will be for him if you and the parent step outside the room briefly. We reassure the child that we will be just outside the room and he can open the door if he needs us.

4. *Videotape Sessions:* We videotape the play sessions for several

reasons. By reviewing the tape, parents can more fully explore their interactions with their children, and they can see the progress they have made toward the goals.

Phase 4: Drawing the Family into the Frame of Play. Our goal is to address specific problem areas for the parents and to increase positive interactions with the child through play. To that end, we focus the process on these three steps:

1. *Expand Play:* Many times we have found that families do not engage in play together. When this occurs, we model play techniques for the parents, including following the child's lead in play and expanding the play. There are many benefits to family play, including increasing the positive, nurturing time between parent and child and helping the parent learn how to "read" the child and attend to the child's desires.

2. *Develop Strategies:* Developing strategies to try with the child is a combination of things the parent has already tried that worked well and brainstorming about other strategies. Once the problems have been identified, the parent is invited to notice times when he did not engage in abusive behavior and used alternative behaviors that worked well. Having the sessions on tape allows the parent-therapist team to observe these times more closely and discuss the experience. You and the parent also may engage in listing other ways of responding to the child's behavior.

3. *Model Alternative Behaviors:* In addition to expanding on the behaviors described by the parent, you may also model appropriate responses to the child and encourage the parent to try some new behaviors. For example, you can model how putting the toys away can be a fun game or a friendly competition (for example, "Let's see if we can get the blocks into the can from here," or "Let's see if you can put the blocks away before I get all the furniture put away"). You might also model giving the child options as a means of obtaining compliance.

Phase 5: Increasing an Empathic Response to the Child. We work with the parents to help them acknowledge their abusive behaviors as a means of discontinuing these behaviors and acquiring empathy for their child. There are two steps in this process:

1. *Acknowledge Abusive Behaviors:* It is important to the success of the therapy for the parent to be able to acknowledge abusive behaviors and accept responsibility for past and future behaviors. Certainly we have found this is difficult for most parents. The key to this step is to explore the parent's own childhood experiences, as this allows the parent to recognize and identify with the child's experience. Acknowledging abusive behaviors generally takes time and occurs in the course of several therapy sessions. We encourage the parent to apologize to the child for their abusive behaviors and ensure the child's future safety.

2. *Increase Empathy for the Child:* Through the acknowledgment of their abusive behavior and also, perhaps, becoming aware of their own past history of abuse, the parents may become better able to take on the child's perspective and appreciate the effect of the abuse on the child. Even a parent who did not face abuse as a child is likely to have had some experience as a child in which he or she was not cared for properly or someone more powerful placed his or her needs above the child's.

Phase 6: Progress Reports and Termination. As we move toward the close of therapy, we may be evaluating therapeutic effectiveness and deciding whether the family should reunify and whether therapy should continue.

If the family is being followed by juvenile court, you will need to submit progress reports regarding progress. These reports will likely address issues of reunification in the cases in which the child has been removed. We have found that even if the child has been returned to the home and the therapy is no longer mandated, the family may continue to benefit from therapy. We determine with the families as to when termination should take place and plan accordingly.

Because this therapy is quite intense (frequently we meet at least twice a week—once with the parents and once for the play session—over the course of a year), we have found that the relationship with the therapist becomes very important for all the family members. Termination should be planned well in advance. We use the last month to review progress and plan for the future. We also discuss the possibility of returning to treatment in the future. We like to remain available to the families if other issues emerge in the future.

MUNCHAUSEN BY PROXY

CHARLIE

At 3:05 A.M. the apnea monitor in Charlie's room goes off. The nursing staff rush in to find Ms. Gordon reviving her three-month-old infant. It is the third time the monitor has gone off this week. The nurse takes Charlie from his mother's arms and after careful evaluation finds that he is once again breathing normally. The on-call physician is paged to perform a complete examination of the child and obtain immediate blood gases. Charlie has an extensive history of numerous apnea episodes, but physicians have not been able to determine the etiology of these episodes. Ms. Gordon is constantly at Charlie's bedside and appears exhausted. The nursing staff bring her a cup of coffee and praise her efforts once again in reviving Charlie.

Later that week, a hidden video camera reveals Ms. Gordon placing a small piece of plastic wrap over Charlie's mouth and nose in order to stop his breathing.

Munchausen by proxy (MBP) is a form of abuse in which a caretaker (usually a parent) falsifies (which may include fabrication or inducement of) physical or psychological symptoms on behalf of another person, usually the person's child, such that the person is considered ill or impaired in order to meet the psychological needs of the caretaker. Professional knowledge of this form of abuse has increased over the past decade, but few of us have experience with it. Similar to other forms of abuse, the parent may not be forthcoming with the acknowledgment of the abusive behaviors. We have implemented a similar treatment program as already described in this chapter in cases of MBP, with medical monitoring added as a mandatory part of any plan in which the child is reunified with the parent. In the medical monitoring, one physician is aware of the alleged MBP and acts as the gatekeeper for any of the children's medical appointments.

We have found that by attempting to understand the parent's childhood as well as adult experiences, we (and the parent) have a more informed and perhaps empathic understanding of what led to the child abuse. This does not mean that we excuse the abusive behavior; rather we are better able to help the parent take control and responsibility for these behaviors. Nor does it mean that we do not get angry. Sometimes we do. However, just as we attempt to help the parents understand and respect the child's experience and not resort to abusive behaviors, we also attempt to understand the abusive parent's experience, notice competencies, and seek support from others when we are experiencing angry or upsetting feelings.

Although we have both worked with parents who were unable to place their child's needs above their own, this is rarely the case. We have found that most parents love their children and are invested in providing good parenting. Despite this goal, some children have been returned to their parents only to receive further abuse. We must continue to examine our reunification practices to protect children adequately and evaluate and refine our treatments in order to provide the best possible treatment to these families.

NOTES

P. 159, *Recent novels such as* . . . Cradle to Grave: Hickey, C., Lighty, T., & O'Brien, J. (1996). *Goodbye my little ones.* New York: Penguin Books; Egginton, J. (1989). *From cradle to grave.* New York: Jove Books.

P. 161, *premature and medically compromised, physically handicapped . . . as particular targets for maltreatment:* National Center on Child Abuse and Neglect. (1994). *State statutes related to child abuse and neglect: 1994.* Washington, DC: U.S. Department of Health and Human Services.

P. 161, *The etiology of abusive behavior is multidetermined:* Belsky, J. (1978). Three theoretical models of child abuse: A critical review. *International Journal of Child Abuse and Neglect, 2,* 27–49.

P. 161, *Jay Belsky contends that there is no one pathway:* Belsky, J. (1993). Etiology of child maltreatment: A developmental-ecological analysis. *Psychological Bulletin, 114*(3), 413–434.

P. 161, *Maxfield and Widom found in a prospective study:* Maxfield, M. G., & Widom, C. S. (1996). The cycle of violence: Revisited 6 years later. *Archives of Pediatrics and Adolescent Medicine, 150*(4), 390–395.

P. 162, *maltreating parents have been observed to interact less frequently with their infants:* Burgess R. L., & Conger, R. D. (1978). Family interaction in abusive, neglectful, and normal families. *Child Development, 49,* 1163–1173.

P. 162, *interactions that do occur are characterized by less supportiveness:* Egeland, B., Breitenbucher, M., & Rosenberg, D. (1980). Prospective study of the significance of life stress in the etiology of child abuse. *Journal of Consulting and Clinical Psychology, 48,* 195–205.

P. 162, *more negativity, both verbal and nonverbal:* Bousha, D. M., & Twentyman, C. T. (1984). Mother-child interactional style in abuse, neglect, and control groups: Naturalistic observations in the home. *Child Development, 93,* 106–114.

P. 163, *Maltreated infants are less able to derive comfort:* Aber, J. L., Allen, J. P., Carlson, V., & Cicchetti, D. (1989). The effects of maltreatment on development during early childhood: Recent studies and their theoretical, clinical, and policy implications. In D. Cicchetti & V. Carlson (Eds.), *Child maltreatment: Theory and research on the causes and consequences of child abuse and neglect.* New York: Cambridge University Press.

P. 163, *Bowlby suggested that an infant's survival:* Bowlby, J. (1969). *Attachment and loss, Vol. 1: Attachment.* New York: Basic Books.

P. 163, *infant patterns of attachment are tied to the behavior of the caregivers:*

Ainsworth, M. D. S., Blehar, M. C., Waters, E., & Wall, S. (1978). *Patterns of attachment.* Hillsdale, NJ: Erlbaum.

P. 163, *anxious attachment:* Crittenden, P. M., & Ainsworth, M. D. S. (1989). Child maltreatment and attachment theory. In D. Cicchetti & V. Carlson (Eds.), *Child maltreatment: Theory and research on the causes and consequences of child abuse and neglect.* New York: Cambridge University Press.

P. 163, *Both abused and neglected infants, toddlers, and preschoolers:* Egeland, B., & Sroufe, L. A. (1981). Attachment and early maltreatment. *Child Development, 11,* 77–92.

P. 163, *show such stress-induced behaviors as stereotyped reactions:* Crittenden, P. M. (1985). Maltreated infants: Vulnerability and resilience. *Journal of Child Psychology and Psychiatry, 26,* 85–96.

P. 164, *development of the toddler's and preschooler's sense of self:* Pipp-Siegel, S., Easterbrooks, M. A., Brown, S. R., & Harmon, R. J. (1995). The relationship between infants' self/mother knowledge and three attachment categories. *Infant Mental Health Journal, 16*(3), 221–232.

P. 164, *Schneider-Rosen and Cicchetti found:* Schneider-Rosen, K., & Cicchetti, D. (1984). The relationship between affect and cognition in maltreated infants: Quality of attachment and the development of visual self-recognition. *Child Development, 55,* 731–746.

P. 164, *preschoolers with anxious attachment patterns . . . dysfunctional relationships with peers:* Lieberman, A. (1977). Preschoolers' competence with a peer: Relationships with attachment and peer experience. *Child Development, 48,* 1277–1287.

P. 164, *J. Lawrence Aber, Joseph Allen, Vicki Carlson, and Dante Cicchetti reported:* Aber, J. L., Allen, J. P., Carlson, V., & Cicchetti, D. (1989). The effects of maltreatment on development during early childhood: Recent studies and their theoretical, clinical, and policy implications. In D. Cicchetti & V. Carlson (Eds.), *Child maltreatment: Theory and research on the causes and consequences of child abuse and neglect.* New York: Cambridge University Press.

P. 164, *Maltreated preschoolers appear to subordinate their desire:* Aber, J. L., & Allen, J. P. (1987). The effects of maltreatment on young children's socioemotional development: An attachment theory perspective. *Developmental Psychology, 23,* 406–414.

P. 164, *Maltreated children have been found . . . disturbed peer relationships:* Mueller, E., & Silverman, N. (1989). Peer relations in maltreated children. In D. Cicchetti & V. Carlson (Eds.), *Child maltreatment: Theory and research on the causes and consequences of child abuse and neglect.* New York: Cambridge University Press.

P. 164, *more likely to react to their age-mates . . . provocative responses:* Main, M., & George, C. (1985). Response of abused and disadvantaged toddlers to distress in agemates: A study in the day care setting. *Developmental Psychology, 21,* 407–412.

P. 164, *neglected children are more likely to withdraw from social interactions:* Hoffman-Plotkin, D., & Twentyman, C. T. (1984). A multimodal assessment of behavioral and cognitive deficits in abused and neglected preschoolers. *Child Development, 55,* 794–802.

P. 165, *they respond to their peers . . . likelihood of further interactions:* Mueller, E., & Silverman, N. (1989). Peer relations in maltreated children. In D. Cicchetti & V. Carlson (Eds.), *Child maltreatment: Theory and research on the causes and consequences of child abuse and neglect* (pp. 529–578). New York: Cambridge University Press.

P. 165, *maltreated preschoolers did not show greater difficulties in interpersonal aggression:* Aber, J. L., Allen, J. P., Carlson, V., & Cicchetti, D. (1989). The effects of maltreatment on development during early childhood: Recent studies and their theoretical, clinical, and policy implications. In D. Cicchetti & V. Carlson (Eds.), *Child maltreatment: Theory and research on the causes and consequences of child abuse and neglect.* New York: Cambridge University Press.

P. 168, *play also permits the child to achieve distance from reality:* Piaget, J. (1962). *Play dreams and imitation in childhood.* New York: International Universities Press.

P. 170, *Specific toys serve to stimulate particular kinds of play:* Axline, W. (1947). *Play therapy.* Boston: Houghton Mifflin.

P. 171, *Parental Acceptance Scoring System:* Rothbaum, F., & Schneider-Rosen, K. (1991). *Parental acceptance scoring manual: A system for assessing interaction between parents and their young children.* Unpublished manuscript. Tufts University, Medford, MA, and Boston College.

P. 171, *Dyadic Connection–Separation Scoring System:* Brown, S. R., Pipp, S., Martz, C., & Waring, R. (1993). Connection and separation in the infant-mother dyad: Patterns of touch and use of interpersonal space. *Infant Mental Health Journal, 14*(4), 317–329.

P. 176, *The family play technique:* Griff, M. D. (1983). Family play therapy. In C. E. Schaefer & K. J. O'Connor (Eds.), *Handbook of play therapy* (pp. 65–75). New York: Wiley.

CHAPTER

8

FEEDING DISORDERS

Carolyn A. Anderson and James Lock

JASON

Jason, an engaging, highly verbal two-and-a-half-year-old, was referred to our clinic for evaluation of feeding problems by a pediatric gastroenterologist, who found some minor medical problems but nothing to explain the severity of Jason's symptoms. Jason had failed to gain weight over a long period of time, and recently he began to lose weight when he should be growing. His parents reported that Jason often refused to eat, vomited frequently during the day when he did eat, gagged on his food, and frequently complained of stomach pain. Mealtimes were a battleground, with Jason refusing to eat and expressing anger toward his parents and Jason's parents trying desperately to get him to eat. They tried cajoling him and distracting him, but as their anxiety and frustration increased, they resorted to punishing Jason for failing to eat and finally tried force-feeding him with a bottle of formula.

Jason's mother had primary responsibility for his care and felt that all her time was taken up by her attempts to feed him. Nothing seemed to help, and she expressed a strong sense of failure as a parent as well as resentment of the child for his difficult behavior. She felt that she had little support from her husband, who worked long hours, and she was socially isolated.

After an outpatient evaluation, Jason was hospitalized because of his continuing weight loss, and we were able to work intensively and successfully with him and his family in that setting.

∾

We are a child psychologist and a psychiatrist who practice in a university setting. We treat our patients with feeding disorders in inpatient and outpatient settings. Like many of our colleagues who treat young children, much of our work also necessarily involves helping parents. Thus in addition to individual play therapy and individual behavioral approaches, we employ parental and family therapy as key parts of our treatment of young children with eating disorders.

In many important ways, Jason is typical of the preschool-age children that we see with feeding disorders. Problems with feeding are relatively common among this age group. Most, however, are relatively transient in nature and do not have lasting effects on the child's development, and so they rarely come to our attention as mental health professionals. Problems with feeding are defined as disorders when they are long-lasting and have notable effects on the child's growth and development.

In young children, the term *Feeding Disorder* rather than *Eating Disorder* is used to capture the dyadic, interactional nature of the problems. By definition, then, these disorders are conceptualized as related to the interaction of the parent and the child rather than simply belonging to the child.

In young children, the development of behaviors such as feeding takes place within the context of relationships with caregivers. According to attachment theory, the security of early attachments to primary caregivers has profound implications for social and emotional development. Emotional and behavioral disorders in young children are viewed as more likely when there are problems in the attachment relationship. Secure relationships between parent and infant develop in the context of responsive parenting. Parents may not be able to provide such parenting because of their own experiences with attachment relationships, stressful circumstances, or psychopathology. Some infants may be more difficult to respond to as well, because of a difficult temperament, medical illness, or other issues. In most cases, infant-parent problems result from a mismatch between what the infant needs and what the parents can provide.

Feeding disorders are most often a symptom of a larger problem within the attachment relationship, and it is important to diagnose and treat feeding disorders within this context. In addition, food and eating are very basic behaviors and are therefore subject to being used symbolically to express a variety of emotional problems. Therefore, as clinicians, we view these problems as specific feeding problems but also seek to help with whatever other problems they may signify. In treatment, we then work toward both behavior change and resolution of these underlying problems.

TYPES OF FEEDING DISORDERS

DSM-IV has three categories of feeding disorders in infants and young children: Feeding Disorder of Infancy or Early Childhood, Rumination Disorder, and Pica.

Feeding Disorder of Infancy and Early Childhood

Most of the children we see fall into the category of Feeding Disorder of Infancy and Early Childhood. To meet criteria for this disorder, the child must have a problem with feeding that results in failure to eat adequately, leading to weight loss or failure to gain adequate weight. The problem must be present for at least one month and not be fully explained by a gastrointestinal or other medical problem. This category is specifically designed for infants and young children; symptoms must begin before age six. Cases formerly labeled as nonorganic failure to thrive would be given this diagnostic label, but other problems of feeding, such as those described in Jason's case, would also receive this diagnosis.

About 1 to 5 percent of pediatric hospital admissions are for failure to gain adequate weight, and up to half of these problems are not caused by any apparent organic etiology. This type of problem may exist in an otherwise healthy child or may coexist with developmental delays or other neuroregulatory disorders such as sleep-wake disturbances.

Rumination Disorder

Rumination Disorder is defined as the repeated regurgitation and rechewing of food in an infant or child that lasts for at least one month and develops after a period of normal functioning. The diagnosis is not given if the behavior is explained by a medical condition or if the symptoms occur as part of an eating disorder or as part of Mental Retardation or a Pervasive Developmental Disorder unless it is sufficiently severe to warrant independent clinical attention. The onset of this disorder is usually between three and twelve months of age and may occur more frequently in males than females. Overall, Rumination Disorder appears to be uncommon. The disorder is of concern because it frequently leads to weight loss, slow growth, and poor nutrition.

Pica

In Pica, children repeatedly eat nonnutritive substances, for a period of at least one month. In younger children, these substances are typically paint, plaster, string, hair, or cloth. This disorder usually begins in infancy and often remits spontaneously in early childhood, although in some children it continues into early adolescence. Pica is an associated feature of Pervasive Developmental Disorder and Mental Retardation, and it should be diagnosed in children with these diagnoses only if the symptoms are severe enough to warrant independent clinical attention. It is not diagnosed if the substances are consumed as part of a culturally sanctioned practice.

The prevalence of Pica is unknown, but many think it may be underdiagnosed in preschool-age children. Children with Pica need careful medical evaluation because of the possibility that it may lead to nutritional deficits or other medical complications such as lead poisoning.

Diagnostic Issues

Our clinical experience, as well as that of others, suggests that the current classification system is inadequate to describe the complexity of feeding problems in young children. Within the category of Feeding Disorder of Infancy and Early Childhood, for example, there may be cases of widely differing presentations and etiology. Other cases of feeding problems are difficult to classify in the current system.

We have seen a number of cases where the feeding problems are clearly posttraumatic in nature, secondary to negative experiences with medical procedures or with choking or gagging. For example, a four-year-old girl recently presented with food refusal that began after she had choked on a piece of hard candy, which she had eaten contrary to her parents' instructions. Treatment for this feeding disorder involved processing of the child's reactions to the traumatic event through brief play therapy as well as the gradual introduction of solid foods combined with behavioral rewards for the child and psychological support for the parents.

Children may also develop feeding disorders when they have not had enough experience with eating during normal critical periods for developing these skills. Often this occurs because of necessary medical interventions; for example, a five-year-old we recently saw had difficulty with eating enough and letting her parents know when she was hungry or thirsty. It turns out that she had had extensive medical intervention in her early years and had been tube-fed until age three; she continued to have tremendous difficulty with feeding in spite of supportive interactions with her family.

Another type of feeding disorder, not captured by the current diagnostic system, is pathological overfeeding, which is thought to be relatively rare but may have serious consequences for the child's health and development.

EVALUATION

In our evaluations of young children with feeding disorders, a multidisciplinary approach is critical. Evaluation of feeding behavior is a complex process that crosses disciplinary lines. In most cases, the child and family are seen by professionals in mental health, pediatrics, pediatric gastrointestinal (GI), nutrition, and occupational therapy. The pediatric and pediatric GI evaluation depends on the level and type of symptoms but is typically thorough and careful. The evaluation by the mental health professional includes a careful feeding history, as well as a general developmental history, a mental status exam, and information from the parents about their own issues and symptoms.

Medical Evaluation

In making the diagnosis of a feeding disorder, establishing the role of organic causes is critically important, and a thorough medical evaluation is always warranted. The goal of such an evaluation should be to search for an organic etiology and to evaluate the child's health status as a guide to decisions about the level of medical intervention needed to protect the child. A diagnosis of a Feeding Disorder is not given if the organic etiology completely explains the problem. These pediatric evaluations are often difficult and inconclusive. Complicating the picture is the fact that both an organic and a psychological etiology may coexist.

In many of the cases we see, there are organic problems, but they are minor and not sufficient to explain the severity of the feeding problem. In these cases, a Feeding Disorder diagnosis is given, and the organic difficulties are taken into account during the treatment. When a severe parent-child interaction problem is suspected, the diagnosis of a Feeding Disorder is often aided by an inpatient hospitalization. If the child begins to gain weight when feeding is supervised by others rather than the parent, this may confirm the Feeding Disorder diagnosis.

Mental Health Evaluation

In taking the feeding history, the mental health professional begins from birth, including breast-feeding and bottle feeding, the transition to solids, and the child's learning to self-feed, as well as the parents' experiences with these transitions. The feeding history is important in helping to identify possible dynamic issues that may be contributing to the problem. For example, in Jason's case, the problems began during the transition to solids and worsened later when he should have been learning to feed himself. We hypothesized in this case that separation and autonomy issues were central and explored these during the treatment.

We also evaluate the child's mental status, paying particular attention to the child's affect and cognition. Children with feeding disorders often present as regressed emotionally and developmentally, and other behavioral issues such as aggression may be apparent. Other children with feeding disorders appear bright and competent in other areas, with more isolated problems around feeding.

During the evaluation, we observe parent-child interactions during a meal as well as at other times. At times we may videotape these interactions to use later in treatment as a way to help the parents view their own behavior more clearly. During the evaluation phase, it can also be useful to observe the child being fed by someone other than the parents, for example, another professional or another family member, to see whether there are marked differences in the child's feeding behavior. The mental health professional will also observe other parent-child interactions, such as the parent and child playing together. This interaction provides information about the parent-child relationships outside the feeding situation and assists in the assessment of the family dynamics.

A psychologist may also decide to test the child to obtain information about the child's developmental level. In the case of a child with developmental delays, this information can be useful in shaping both the parents' and the treatment team's expectations of the child. The nutritionist meets with the family to explore the child's typical caloric intake and feeding patterns, and also provides the team with an estimate of the child's actual caloric needs. Whenever possible, the family is asked to keep a careful food record to facilitate this process.

Inpatient Evaluation

At times, inpatient hospitalization is necessary for the diagnosis and treatment of severe feeding disorders. Usually the determining factor about whether to hospitalize the child depends on the child's medical condition and therefore whether a slower, less intensive approach will be safe enough for the child. Also, previous outpatient treatment failure is a strong argument to try an inpatient approach.

Typically, we use the first few days of an inpatient stay as a period of more intensive assessment of the feeding issues. A careful food record is kept by the nursing staff, to provide us and the nutritionist with accurate information about the child's intake of food. Sometimes we find that the parent has either exaggerated or underestimated the child's usual intake, so this information can be invaluable to treatment planning. Nurses who are trained in both psychiatric and medical nursing can provide observations of parent-child interactions throughout the day in different settings. During an inpatient stay, the pediatric specialists continue to assess organic problems that complicate the feeding problem.

TREATMENTS

Our approach to the treatment of feeding disorders, like our evaluation process, is interdisciplinary and usually combines several different modalities. For such treatment to be successful, a high level of collaboration and communication among professionals is critically important. Treatment of feeding disorders may occur on either an inpatient or outpatient basis. We find that outpatient approaches tend to be slower getting started but are effective and may be less disruptive to the child and the rest of the family. They are also less costly, and so may be more likely to be authorized and paid for by insurance companies. In terms of treatment, similar techniques are used in both settings, but the level of intensity varies.

Overview of the Treatment Process

Once we have completed our initial assessment of a child with a feeding disorder, we begin to put together a treatment plan in collaboration with the treatment team. If we determine that mental health intervention is needed, this typically includes dyadic work on parent-child interactions both within and outside the feeding situation. In addition, individual work with the parents is initiated for education and support, as well as exploration of psychodynamic issues that are affecting their parenting. Individual work with the child usually involves behavioral interventions to support improved feeding and may include play therapy to help the child process feelings about the feeding issues. Other services such as nutrition education for the parents and work with the occupational therapist on any oral-motor problems in the child will also be provided by other team members.

Often in the early stages of treatment, a nutritional formula such as Pediasure or Ensure is used for feeding rather than solid food. This is used as a way of changing established patterns of eating, so that new patterns can be put in place. More important, this type of diet provides balanced nutrition and simplifies monitoring of caloric intake. Over time, the child can gradually be advanced to solid food.

When we see that the interactions between parent and child around feeding are grossly maladaptive, we may recommend that the parents remove themselves from the feeding process altogether in the initial stages of treatment. In the hospital, this means that nursing staff take over the feeding. On an outpatient basis, it requires more creativity, but we work to find relatives or other support people who can help.

We choose this course for several reasons. First, it is an opportunity to give the child a different experience with feeding and begin to change maladaptive patterns. Ideally, the child can be provided with regular mealtimes and supportive, responsive interactions around feeding. Second, if the child is severely malnourished, we may be able to change the pattern more quickly in this way and thus avoid more invasive medical interventions. If such interventions are needed, we structure them in such a way that needed therapeutic work around feeding can still be done with the child. Finally, taking the responsibility of feeding away from the parents on a temporary basis can relieve their anxiety about the child's health and provide an opening for therapeutic work. Some parents become anxious and defensive in the face of such an intervention and may need considerable support to be able to follow this treatment recommendation. For such parents, a combination of psychoeducation, emotional support, and exploration of psychodynamic issues seems to be helpful.

After some improvement has been noted in the child and a better alliance is formed with the parent, we gradually reintroduce the parents into the feeding process. Initially we sit with the parents as they observe a feeding by another person and discuss with them their reactions. Parents often have mixed feelings about the other person's success; although pleased by the child's progress, they often feel hurt that the child was not able to make such progress with them. We may also sit with parents while they watch a videotape of themselves feeding their child. We use this process to help them view their own behavior more objectively and thus gain greater insight into their own contributions to the feeding problem. This intervention is also helpful in eliciting parents' feelings about feeding their child.

We ask the parents to take over feeding gradually, coaching and modeling appropriate behaviors for them. With preschoolers, this often means that the parents need to learn to provide the child with more independence with certain eating behaviors (for example, the child feeds himself or herself) and more support with others (for example, providing regular, structured mealtimes with fewer interruptions). When the parents are able to have some success in managing the child's eating, the family is ready for outpatient management.

Dyadic Therapy

Dyadic therapy, also called parent-child therapy, is central to our work with feeding disorders in both the inpatient and outpatient setting. In this type of therapy, we work with the young child and the parents together, with the goal of changing maladaptive interactions and strengthening the attachment relationship between the parent and child.

The whole relationship between Jason and his parents had become focused around feeding. Their interactions had become highly aversive, and they became angrier and angrier with each other. Initial goals in the dyadic therapy were to provide them both with a different experience in the relationship, so the sessions were structured around play rather than feeding, and we supported Jason's mother in beginning to interact more positively with him.

In our experience, a central issue in feeding disorders is the parents' difficulty reading and interpreting their child's cues correctly and then responding appropriately. Preschoolers communicate with both words and actions, and parents may have difficulty attending to both. For example, parents may not see their child's cues for hunger and satiety, and they may therefore respond inappropriately to the child's needs. In dyadic therapy, we help the parents learn to understand their child's communication, through techniques such as interpreting for the parents and coaching them to respond appropriately.

The most striking example we have seen of this was in a case of overfeeding, in which the child would begin to shake his head "no" to indicate that he had eaten enough. The mother would completely ignore these clear signals and continue to offer him spoonfuls of food. After a few urgings, he would give in and eat more, in order to please her, and the cycle began again on the next bite. Treatment involved coaching the mother to observe her child's signals and respond appropriately, in this case taking the food away and switching to another activity when he indicated that he was ready to stop eating.

Also using the dyadic approach, we work with parents on helping their preschool-age child to develop appropriate autonomy. Parents who face difficulties with feeding tend to become anxious, and this often leads to attempts to control the child's behavior. Overcontrolling behavior on the part of the parents leads to increased oppositionality by the child in a struggle for autonomy, and the feeding disorder often worsens. Parents and children may then engage in increasingly more negative and coercive interactions. In other cases, children may passively accept the parental control. In dyadic therapy, then, our goal is to help the parent back off and allow the child to develop appropriate independence with feeding and other issues. For example, if a parent of a preschooler is still spoon-feeding a child who is capable of feeding himself or herself, we use the dyadic therapy to model appropriate encouragement of independence and coach the parent to encourage the child's development of feeding skills. This was true in Jason's case; turning the spoon over to him led to much improvement in his intake in a relatively short time. These issues of control may also extend to other areas of parent-child interaction, and these can be addressed as well.

The issue of limit setting can be worked on in dyadic therapy. Some parents are unable to set appropriate limits with their preschool children, and this worsens the feeding problem. For example, children may refuse to sit at the table and eat, or parents may allow the child to hit them without responding. With this type of problem, we use dyadic therapy to model setting firm, consistent limits and to coach parents on following through without being punitive.

For many families with feeding disorders, the feeding issues have pervaded all aspects of their relationship with their child. Parents tell us that they spend all day trying to get their child to eat, and for many this may literally be true. As part of the dyadic therapy, we work on helping the parents to develop a positive relationship with their child outside the feeding context. This often involves teaching the parents to play with their child without letting the feeding problems interfere and helping the parents to see how much the child enjoys and needs this type of interaction with them.

Establishing positive interactions between parent and child can help to ameliorate some of the damage that has been done through the feeding difficulties. At the same time, we work to help the child and parents communicate with each other in different ways, so that food and feeding issues are no longer used for communicating basic emotional issues in the relationship.

Therapy with the Parents

We also work with the parents separately from the child to support their progress. This always encompasses some education for the parents about developmental issues and the feeding problems, and it may include helping the parents to understand any medical problems the child has that may be contributing to the feeding problem. Parents also need support to manage their own feelings about the child's feeding problems. For example, parents may be anxious, they may feel angry at the child for having so many difficulties, or they may feel incompetent for their perceived failure to manage their child's feeding. The meaning of the child's feeding problems to the parent is always important to explore.

Many parents of children with feeding problem are still struggling with attachment issues from their own childhoods and may be reenacting these issues with their children.

Jason's mother began to view her son's problems as volitional and became angry and resentful. She then began force-feeding her child in a punitive manner and needed assistance in seeing that this intervention came out of her own anger rather than to help her child. In further exploration, she identified that control struggles in this interaction were more extreme versions of the difficulties that she had in her own family of origin.

For parents with more serious psychopathology, we may recommend ongoing individual therapy. Anxiety disorders and depression are especially common in parents of children with feeding disorders. We recommend marital therapy when couples issues are affecting the feeding process. One mother, for example, recently identified that her anger at her husband for working long hours and leaving her with all of the responsibility for their child was in part fueling the anger she expressed at the child during feeding interactions. Marital therapy may help the couple resolve these issues, by dealing with the issues directly rather than allowing them to be expressed through the child.

Individual Therapy with the Child

In our individual work with children with feeding disorders, we take several different approaches. Behavioral methods are almost always part of the intervention. When a child is refusing food in

an oppositional manner, clear behavioral expectations and immediate tangible rewards for appropriate food consumption may
help to change this behavior. One dual-purpose reward that we
have used is a special playtime with the parent following a meal-
time when the child consumes a minimum quantity of food.
This has the effect of rewarding the child for improved behavior as well as providing a chance for positive interaction between
parent and child. With preschool children, any rewards should
be immediate and concrete, so that the child is able to make the
connection between the desired behavior and the rewards. Stickers are easy to administer, inexpensive, and often highly valued
by young children, especially when given along with praise.

The therapeutic structure we developed for Jason and his mother
was for them to engage in a special playtime before and after each
meal. Stickers were also used initially; Jason received one after every
few bites. Over time, the positive aspects of the play sessions became
part of the feeding interactions as well, and Jason and his mother
became more playful and positive in their interactions with each
other. Jason increased the quantity of food that he ate at each meal,
and he also appeared to enjoy the mealtimes that previously had
been aversive experiences.

Encouraging the child to play with food is often a part of the
intervention with the child. Many children with feeding problems have not experienced the explorations of food that are part
of normal development. For this reason, we encourage our
patients to explore different textures of foods and to play with
the food without restrictions in the initial stages of treatment.
This allows the child to have a more positive experience with
food itself and may allow him or her to move to the next stage,
which is to begin eating the food rather than just playing with it.

Many parents of children with feeding disorders have difficulty allowing the food play and are concerned about how messy it is or want the child to eat rather than play. Parents may need support around these issues and need to understand the important role this play often has in the treatment.

When the feeding problem appears to be a more classically conditioned response in which an aversive event or stimulus has become paired with food, behavioral approaches such as in vivo desensitization can be useful. Here, the anxiety-producing stimulus is gradually introduced while using techniques to help manage the anxiety. For a child with a strong food aversion, foods can be introduced little by little with support for the child's anxiety. The child can be encouraged to play with the food and touch it, and then new foods can be gradually introduced. Often we begin with liquids, then move to soft foods, and then on to solids. Amounts can be gradually increased as the child is ready.

Individual play therapy can be useful in conjunction with the other interventions. Play therapy seems to be especially useful when the child appears to be angry with the parent around feeding issues or when there has been some type of traumatic experience that needs to be processed. Play therapy works by helping the child resolve issues through representation in play. In play therapy with these children, we use plastic food and dishes as well as play with a dollhouse or other figures to elicit the feeding issues more directly. For example, a child may be asked to feed a doll in order to work out some of his or her feelings about feeding.

Medication

For many childhood disorders, psychotropic medications may play a role in the treatment. Our understanding of the psychotropic medications in feeding and eating disorders is still developing. There may be some important roles for serotonic reuptake inhibitors (like Prozac) in the future. For now, psychotropic medication use is indicated only when there is a clear secondary diagnosis, like an anxiety disorder or depression, that would be likely to respond to these medications. With infants and toddlers, we have only a few data to support medications even in these instances. For now, psychotropic medications will rarely play a role in the treatment of feeding disorders in young children

Additional Interventions

Interventions by other professionals on our team often complement our efforts. The nutritionist provides ongoing education to the parent about the child's nutritional needs, and this work can be coordinated with our education efforts. Individual work by our occupational therapist can be powerful in providing a different feeding experience for the child. The occupational therapy intervention is especially important when the child has oral-motor problems or sensitivities that complicate the feeding process. In these cases, the occupational therapist uses structured interventions to decrease oral sensitivity or to retrain the oral-motor musculature to work more normally.

COLLABORATION AND TRANSFERENCE ISSUES

Most of our work with children with feeding disorders occurs in the context of a multidisciplinary team that works collaboratively with the child and family. We are fortunate to work in a setting where such collaborative relationships are the norm, but still find that we need to pay continuing attention to the issue of communication and to hold frequent meetings to facilitate joint treatment planning. In situations where such relationships do not exist, the responsibility often falls on the mental health professional to create such relationships and to play a central role in managing the case. Frequent contact by telephone with each

204 Treating Preschool Children

member of the treatment team is critical. Whenever possible, we recommend a face-to-face treatment planning meeting upon initiation of intervention.

In treating preschoolers, the cooperation and involvement of the family is critically important, and we put a great deal of effort into enlisting the family's participation and continuing to support them throughout the treatment process. It is important to approach families in a respectful, nonblaming manner in order to create a good working relationship and decrease defensiveness. Cases where such an alliance is not established are the least likely to improve.

In identifying the need for treatment in these cases, there are several pitfalls. In some of our pediatric colleagues, we have noticed a tendency to focus on medical explanations for the feeding problems and to avoid exploration of possible psychosocial factors until no other possibility remains. In one case of a morbidly obese child, medical intervention and evaluation had continued without success for over a year before the psychiatry service was consulted, in part because the medical professionals involved had difficulty considering the idea that the mother might be part of the problem. The problem turned out to be one of pathological overfeeding, and the child and mother responded well to psychiatric intervention. However, that year of waiting was costly to the child's health and development.

In other cases, the opposite may occur: parents may be blamed for problems that actually have an organic basis. We recently saw a preschooler with Turner's Syndrome, who like all other girls with this genetic disorder, was extremely small for her age. Before the syndrome was finally diagnosed, her mother had been told that she was probably responsible for her child's slow growth because she was underfeeding the child. After worrying about feeding and doing her best to correct the problem for six months, the mother was finally told that her child had Turner's Syndrome, and so the slow growth probably had little to do with feeding. A multidisciplinary team is the best way to avoid these pitfalls, although some mistakes are probably inevitable with such complicated conditions.

CASE MANAGEMENT ISSUES

Case management for feeding problems can be complicated because of the interdisciplinary team involved and the need for coordination. This situation becomes even more complicated when members of the team do not agree about what should be done. In these cases, it often falls to the mental health professional to bring the team together to build consensus. We find that organizing a care conference with the entire treatment team present is the most helpful way to approach this problem. At times, we ask parents to join us at the end of the care conference to meet with the team and discuss our recommendations.

Managed Care

All too often in managed care, insurance coverage plays a role in decisions about evaluation and treatment approaches. For multidisciplinary evaluations, separate authorizations are often needed for the mental health and pediatric components. When mental health benefits are carved out to a different insurance company from the one dealing with the medical benefits, the treatment team may have to work with two separate systems that may have separate contracting arrangements with their institution. In these situations, it helps to work together with the pediatricians to argue the need for a truly multidisciplinary evaluation by a team who can work closely together.

Insurance authorizations are most difficult to obtain when inpatient hospitalization is recommended, because of the high cost. Documentation of imminent risk to the child if he or she is not hospitalized is often needed; the pediatricians are usually best equipped to make this argument based on the child's weight and other medical issues such as dehydration. Also, evidence of past outpatient treatment failure is a good argument for hospitalization.

Sometimes we are unsuccessful in obtaining insurance coverage for an inpatient stay even though we believe that it is the best option for the child. In these cases, we may need to use an outpatient approach with very careful monitoring to ensure the child's safety. We find it useful to set clear criteria for treatment success and failure that are agreed on by the multidisciplinary team prior to beginning the outpatient treatment. These criteria are documented in the chart and clearly communicated to the insurance case manager. If the outpatient treatment is then unsuccessful based on our criteria, we reapproach the insurance company with these data to request inpatient care. Through this process of careful treatment planning and documentation, we are often more successful in obtaining the needed coverage and are then able to provide the child with the recommended treatment.

Considering Out-of-Home Placement

The most difficult issues arise when the question of out-of-home placement must be considered. When parent-child interactions are identified as the cause of a feeding problem that is endangering a child's health and welfare, then the question of abuse and neglect needs to be considered. We find that the line between maladaptive parenting and abuse or neglect is often a fuzzy one, with few clear standards to guide us in cases of feeding disorder. In part, we base our assessment on the degree of risk to the child, as well as the parent's ability to benefit from treatment.

If in our judgment the child is at imminent risk of harm because of pathological feeding behaviors, then it is our responsibility to report the abuse or neglect to the local CPS. We then work with the assigned caseworker to try for the best outcome for the child. Sometimes the agency can be used to compel reluctant parents into treatment and can provide resources for treatment that may not be available otherwise. In a recent case of a child who was failing to gain weight because of inconsistent feeding interactions, we worked with CPS to design a program of parenting training and individual therapy for the parent and medical monitoring of the child. The CPS worker then monitored and enforced the parent's participation in these interventions. In other cases, a relatively brief stay in medical foster care may help the child gain needed weight to get out of medical danger while the parents are in intensive therapy in preparation for the child's return. Unfortunately, such a plan also has the undesirable effect of straining the already insecure attachment between parent and child; nevertheless, it still may be necessary. In the most severe cases, after treatment failure, permanent removal from the home and placement in foster care may be the only safe option for the child. When CPS is involved, we stay in close contact with the worker so that to the degree possible, our clinical judgment is reflected in the decisions that are made.

Because of the long-term effects on growth and development, feeding disorders have the potential to do lasting harm to children. In addition, there is evidence that feeding problems in young children are associated with eating disorder symptoms in adolescence, indicating that some of these children continue to have serious problems around food and eating. For these reasons, diagnosis and treatment of young children with feeding disorders are critically important. Although these cases are complicated in terms of management, they often respond well to intervention, leading to satisfactory outcomes for the children and their families.

NOTES

P. 188, *used to capture the dyadic, interactional nature of the problems:* Benoit, D. (1993). Failure to thrive and feeding disorders. In C. H. Zeanah (Ed.), *Handbook of infant mental health*. New York: Guilford.

P. 188, *According to attachment theory:* Bowlby, J. (1969). *Attachment and loss: Vol. 1: Attachment.* New York: Basic Books; Ainsworth, M. D. S., Blehar, M., Waters, E., & Wall, S. (1978). *Patterns of attachment: A psychological study of the Strange Situation.* Hillsdale, NJ: Erlbaum; Belsky, J., & Nezworski, T. (Eds.). (1988). *Clinical implications of attachment.* Hillsdale, NJ: Erlbaum.

P. 189, *Feeding disorders are most often . . . problem within the attachment relationship:* Chattoor, I., & Egan (1987). Etiology and diagnosis of failure to thrive and growth disorders in infants and children. In J. Noshpitz (Ed.), *Basic Handbook in Child Psychiatry* (Vol. 5). New York: Basic Books.

P. 190, *The onset of this disorder . . . may occur more frequently in males than females:* American Psychiatric Association. (1994). *Diagnostic and statistical manual of mental disorders* (4th ed.). Washington, DC: Author.

P. 191, *Our clinical experience, as well as that of others:* Ramsay, M. (1995). Feeding disorder and failure to thrive. *Infant Psychiatry, 4,* 605–616; Benoit, D. (1993). Failure to thrive and feeding disorders. In C. H. Zeanah (Ed.), *Handbook of Infant Mental Health.* New York: Guilford.

P. 192, *pathological overfeeding, . . . thought to be relatively rare:* Benoit, D. (1993). Failure to thrive and feeding disorders. In C. H. Zeanah (Ed.), *Handbook of Infant Mental Health.* New York: Guilford.

P. 192, *Complicating the picture . . . organic and a psychological etiology may coexist:* Ramsay, M. (1995). Feeding disorder and failure to thrive. *Infant Psychiatry, 4,* 605–616.

P. 207, *feeding problems in young children . . . eating disorder symptoms in adolescence:* Marchi, M., & Cohen, P. (1990). Early childhood eating behaviors and adolescent eating disorder. *Journal of the American Academy of Child and Adolescent Psychiatry, 29,* 112–117.

ABOUT THE AUTHORS

Carolyn A. Anderson, Ph.D., is a staff psychologist and clinical instructor in the Division of Child Psychiatry and Child Development, Stanford University School of Medicine, and she serves as the program director of the Partial Hospitalization Program at Packard Children's Hospital. She is also a staff psychologist at the Children's Health Council in Palo Alto, California. Her research has focused primarily on family interactions and Attention-Deficit/Hyperactivity Disorder. Clinical interests include eating and feeding disorders, family therapy, and evaluation and treatment of preschool-age children.

Anne L. Benham, M.D., is a clinical associate professor of psychiatry and behavioral sciences in the Division of Child Psychiatry and Child Development, Stanford University School of Medicine. She serves as the director of infant psychiatry at the Children's Health Council, Palo Alto, California, where she developed a multidisciplinary program for the evaluation and treatment of young children. She specializes in the areas of attachment disorders, the effects of trauma and loss on young children, and the development of treatment models for toddlers and young preschoolers and their parents. Dr. Benham is a member of the task force of the American Academy of Child and Adolescent Psychiatry (AACAP), which recently completed the Practice Parameters for the Assessment of Infants and Toddlers, and she is the author of a new Infant-Toddler Mental Status Exam, which has been incorporated into this document.

Scott R. Brown is an independent practitioner in Boulder, Colorado. He is currently completing his doctorate at the University of Colorado. He completed his predoctoral internship at Packard Children's Hospital at Stanford. Mr. Brown has conducted research and written extensively in the area of parent-child interaction and child abuse. His clinical and research interests are in the evaluation and treatment of infants, toddlers, and preschoolers and their families, as well as child abuse.

Victor G. Carrion, M.D., is a National Institute of Mental Health Scholar in the Division of Child Psychiatry and Child Development, Stanford University School of Medicine, where he is researching the link between child abuse and dissociation. His interests include the neurophysiological correlates of trauma and victimization and the phases of development in sexual minority youth.

Maria Villalba Devera, M.D., is a clinical instructor of psychiatry and behavioral sciences in the Division of Child Psychiatry and Child Development, Stanford University School of Medicine. She is medical director of the Comprehensive Partial Hospitalization Program at Packard Children's Hospital at Stanford. Dr. Devera directs the pediatric neuropsychiatric outpatient clinic, with special interests in tics and movement disorders, and sleep.

S. Shirley Feldman, Ph.D., teaches in the Division of Child and Psychiatry and Child Development, Stanford University School of Medicine, and served as director of the Stanford Center for the Study of Families, Children, and Youth from 1991 to 1995. Her extensive research on socialization of children and adolescents is contained in books, monographs, and more than one hundred papers. Her interests have focused recently on adolescent development, and she has co-edited the influential volume *At the Threshold: The Developing Adolescent* (1990). She has conducted longitudinal studies that span two important transitions—from childhood into early adolescence, and from late adolescence into adulthood—in which she focuses on family influences on both normal and pathological development (including depression, delinquency, and promiscuity).

Brian N. Kleis, M.D., is the medical director for Midpeninsula Mental Health Group and a clinical instructor in the Division of Child and Psychiatry and Child Development, Stanford University School of Medicine. He is board certified in child, adolescent, and adult psychiatry and specializes in working with youths who have gender identity or sexual orientation issues. He serves on several committees within Stanford Health Services and on the American Academy of Child and Adolescent Psychiatry's Homosexual Issues Committee.

James Lock, Ph.D., M.D., is an assistant professor of child psychiatry in the Division of Child and Psychiatry and Child Development, Stanford University School of Medicine, and medical director of the Comprehensive Pediatric Care Unit at the Packard Children's Hospital at Stanford. Dr. Lock's main research activities have focused on the treatment of major depression and eating disorders in children and adolescents. He has published articles on psychotherapeutic treatment of eating disorders, Attention-Deficit/Hyperactivity Disorder, and sexual development. He serves on a number of local, state, and national committees for the advancement of child psychiatry.

Linda J. Lotspeich, M.D., is an assistant professor of psychiatry in the Division of Child and Psychiatry and Child Development, Stanford University School of Medicine. She is also director of the Pervasive Developmental Disorders Clinic at Children's Health Council, Palo Alto, California. Her publications include chapters on the neurobiology of autism and papers on the genetics of autism. She was a Presidential Scholar of the American Academy of Child and Adolescent Psychiatry and has been awarded several research fellowships. Her clinical work is centered on diagnosis and treatment of children with Pervasive Developmental Disorders and autism, with a special interest in the neurobiology of autism.

Mary J. Sanders, Ph.D., is the director of psychological services and clinical instructor in the Division of Child Psychiatry and Child Development, Stanford University School of Medicine.

Since 1986, she has been at the Packard Children's Hospital at Stanford where she is a specialist in the areas of child abuse and eating disorders. Dr. Sanders has presented nationally in the areas of eating disorders and Munchausen syndrome by proxy.

Richard J. Shaw, M.B., B.S., is an assistant professor in the Division of Child Psychiatry and Child Development, Stanford University School of Medicine. He is also medical director of Consultation-Liaison Services at Packard Children's Hospital at Stanford. His research interests include the study of affect expression, affect recognition in schizophrenia, and the adjustment in children with severe medical illnesses.

Hans Steiner, M.D., is a professor of psychiatry and behavioral sciences in the Division of Child Psychiatry and Child Development, Stanford University School of Medicine. He is a Fellow of the American Psychiatric Association, the American Academy of Child and Adolescent Psychiatry, and the Academy of Psychosomatic Medicine. He received the Outstanding Mentor Award of the American Academy of Child and Adolescent Psychiatry in 1990, 1992, 1993, 1995, and 1996. He also received the Dlin/Fischer Award for significant achievement in clinical research by the Academy of Psychosomatic Medicine in 1993. He is the recipient of the 1996 Joseph B. Goldberger Award in Clinical Nutrition of the American Medical Association. His research and clinical work is concentrated on the adolescent age group. He is an internationally known expert in eating disorders, trauma-related psychopathology, and juvenile delinquency.

Margo Thienemann, M.D., is a clinical assistant professor in the Division of Child Psychiatry and Child Development, Stanford University School of Medicine. She is also the director of the Child and Adolescent Obsessive-Compulsive Disorder Clinic at Stanford University Medical Center and consultant to two special education programs in Palo Alto: the Children's Health Council and the Peninsula Children's Center.

INDEX

Encopresis, 87–89, 99–110; as adjustment disorder, 102; as anger expression, 100, 103, 109; behavioral
treatment for, 104–106; case example of, 88–89; with constipation and
overflow soiling, 89, 101, 104–106,
109; without constipation, 102,
106–108; countertransference issues
with, 108–109; defined, 88, 100;
diet for, 104, 105; difficulties caused
by, 99, 102, 103; *DSM-IV* criteria
for, 100; with emotional problems,
102, 106–109; epidemiology of,
100; etiology of, 100–103; evaluation of, 103–104; hospitalization
for, 105, 106–108; medical evaluation for, 104; mental health evaluation for, 103–104; with
psychopathology, 103; psychosocial
factors in, 100; risky
situations/times for, 101; secondary
emotional problems of, 102; secondary gain of, 103; with stress,
102, 104; treatment of, 104–109;
treatment outcomes of, 109
Enuresis, 87–89, 90–99, 109–110;
alarm systems for, 95–97; associated
with sleep apnea, 78; behavior therapy for, 95–98; bladder training for,
96–97; case example of, 88–89;
defined, 87, 90; development and,
91; difficulties caused by, 93; diurnal, 90; *DSM-IV* criteria for, 90;
epidemiology of, 90; etiology of,
91–93; evaluation of, 93–94; gene,
91; hypnosis for, 97–98; managed
care and, 94; medication for, 98–99;
nocturnal, 90; organic causes of,
92–93; primary, 90; psychoeducation about, 94; psychotherapy for,
99; secondary, 90; sleep disorders
and, 92; stressors and, 91, 92; toilet
training difficulties and, 91, 92;
treatment of, 89, 94–99; types of,
90. *See also* Bed wetting
Environment: attachment disorders

and, 129; encopresis and, 100;
enuresis and, 92; sleep disorders
and, 61; temperament and, 5–7, 25.
See also Family environment
Extinction techniques, for protodys-
somnia sleep problems, 69–70
Extroversion, as temperament trait, 5
Eye contact, 41–42, 54

F

Facial features, in autism, 31, 41
Failure to thrive: abuse/neglect and,
160, 170; attachment disorders and,
123; Feeding Disorder of Infancy
and Early Childhood as, 189–190;
prevalence of, 190. *See also* Feeding
Disorder of Infancy and Early
Childhood; Feeding disorders
Fairy tales, *xv–xvi, xvii*
Falling asleep, difficulty in. *See* Protodyssomnia
Family bed. *See* Co-sleeping
Family environment: and development of psychological/behavioral
difficulties, 1; and goodness of fit
with temperament, 5–7, 25
Family history: of enuresis, 91; of
Pervasive Developmental Disorders, 46. *See also* Genetic influences
Family interview, for Gender Identity
Disorder evaluation, 146–148
Family play technique, 176–181; goal
setting in, 178; goals of, 176; intensity of, 181; intervention planning
in, 177–179; modeling in, 176, 179;
parent-child interaction in, 177;
Parental Acceptance Scoring System use in, 177; in Phase 1-Estab-
lishing a Relationship with the
Family, 177; in Phase 2-Assessing
the Parent-Child Interaction, 177;
in Phase 3-Planning Play Session
Interventions, 177–179; in Phase 4-
Drawing the Family into the Frame
of Play, 179; in Phase 5-Increasing
an Empathic Response to the

Child, 180; in Phase 6-Progress Reports and Termination, 180; phases of, 176–181; problem definition in, 178; progress reports of, 180; step-outs in, 178; structure of, 176; termination of, 180, 181; therapeutic relationship in, 177, 181
Family size, enuresis and, 90
Family therapy: for abusive situations, 175–181; for Gender Identity Disorder, 150–152. *See also* Dyadic psychotherapy; Family play technique
Fathers: and play, 13; and separation anxiety, 13. *See also* Parents
Feeding, and attachment, 12
Feeding Disorder of Infancy or Early Childhood, 189–190; age of onset of, 189; diagnostic criteria for, 189; diagnostic issues of, 191; nonorganic failure to thrive as, 190; prevalence of, 190. *See also* Feeding disorders
Feeding disorders, *xviii*, 187–207; attachment and, 12, 25, 188–189; behavioral techniques for, 200–202; case example of, 187–188; case management issues of, 205–207; diagnosis of, 189–192; diagnosis of, complexity of, 191–192, 204–205; *DSM-IV* categories of, 189; dyadic therapy for, 197–199; versus eating disorders, 188; emotional expression and, 189; etiology of, 191–192; evaluation of, 192–194; food play and, 201–202; hospitalization for, 194, 195–197, 205–206; limit setting and, 199; managed care and, 205–206; medical treatments in etiology of, 191–192; medication for, 202–203; multidisciplinary collaboration in, 203–205; multidisciplinary interventions in, 203; versus normal feeding problems, 188; nutritional formulas for, 195–196; organic etiology of, 192–193, 204–205; organic problems co-

morbidity with, 192–193, 204–205; out-of-home placement for, 206–207; parent involvement/ noninvolvement in feeding and, 196–197; parent misreading child's cues and, 197–198; parent therapy for, 199–200; parent-child interaction and, 188–189, 196; of pathological overfeeding, 192, 204; posttraumatic, 191; rewards for behavior improvement in, 201; safety monitoring for, 206; transference issues in, 203–205; treatment of, 188, 195–203; treatment of, process overview, 195–197; types of, 189–192. *See also* Feeding Disorder of Infancy or Early Childhood; Pica; Rumination Disorder
Feldman, S. S., 1
Films, for therapist immersion, *xvii–xviii*
Fit, goodness of, 5–7, 8, 25, 189
Foster care: age placed in, 18–19; attachment disorders and, 113–114; for attachment disorders, 133–134. *See also* Institutions; Placement, out-of-home
Foxx, A. Z., 85–86, 96
Fragile X Syndrome, 43–44, 45, 49
Fraiberg, S., *xviii*, 130
Frances stories, *xvii*
Frustration, and control of emotions, 22, 23
Fusion, in normal symbiotic phase, 16

G
Gastrocolic reflex, 104
Gatekeeping: and Munchausen by proxy, 182; and Pervasive Developmental Disorders treatment, 55–56. *See also* Managed care
Gender consistency, 141
Gender development, 139–143; normal, 139–142
Gender identity: defined, 139; development of, 139–143
Gender Identity Disorder (GID),

Rumination Disorder, 189, 190; age
of onset of, 190; diagnostic criteria
for, 190; gender differences in, 190.
See also Feeding disorders
Russo, R., 68

S

Safety: guarding, for night terrors, 77;
monitoring for feeding disorders,
206; in play therapy for abused
children, 169–170
Samoan culture, co-sleeping in, 74
San Francisco Bay Area, gatekeepers
in, 55
Sanders, M. J., 159
Schedules, for Pervasive Develop-
mental Disordered children, 51, 53
Schizophrenia, childhood: etiology of,
2; Pervasive Developmental Disor-
ders versus, 42
Schneider-Rosen, K., 164
School. *See* Preschool
School districts, and Pervasive Devel-
opmental Disorders treatment,
55–56
Sears, R., 73
Secure attachment, 15–16, 118, 119.
See also Attachment
Security, and attachment, 11, 13, 115
Seizure Disorder, and autism, 46
Seizures: from DDAVP therapy, 99;
diurnal, 77; nocturnal, 77
Selective serotonin reuptake
inhibitors (SSRIs): for autism
symptoms, 54; for feeding disor-
ders, 202
Self, development of, *xiv–xvi;* abuse
and, 164. *See also* Development
Self-esteem: and attachment, 11; and
encopresis, 102; and Gender Iden-
tity Disorder, 148
Self-hypnosis, for enuresis, 97–98
Self-injurious behaviors, in Pervasive
Developmental Disorders, 40, 54;
medication for, 54

Self-soothing aids, 63; co-sleeping
and, 74–75; cultural variables in,
74. *See also* Transitional objects
Self-soothing capacity, and sleep
problem etiology, 62, 68
Self-stimulation: autistic, 32–33; masturbation, 140
Sendak, M., *xvi*
Sensitivity, of mothers, 18
Sensory fatigue, and encopresis, 89
Separation: distress of, normal, 12;
effects of, and attachment disorders, 120–123, 129; from family, in
fairy tales, *xv–xvi;* due to hospitalization, 120–122; reactions to,
stages of, 121–122. *See also* Loss
Separation anxiety: and normal separation-individuation, 13–14, 17; and
sleep problems, 68. *See also* Anxiety
Separation Anxiety Disorder, 14;
early loss and, 14, 15; Gender
Identity Disorder with, 142,
148–149, 156; separation-individuation difficulties and, 15; temperament and, 25
Separation-individuation, 15, 16–17;
difficulties in, and Separation Anxiety Disorder, 15; stages of, 16–17.
See also Attachment
Sex awareness/activity, development
of, 139–142
Sex identity, defined, 139. *See also*
Gender identity
Sexual abuse: attachment disorders
and, 129; encopresis and, 100; risk
of, in co-sleeping, 73. *See also*
Abuse; Neglect; Trauma
Shaken Baby Syndrome, 160
Shaping technique, for protodyssom-
nia sleep problems, 70
Shaw, R. J., 1, 113
Sickle cell anemia, 93
Siegel, B., 51
Skill-centered play therapy, 168–169,
170. *See also* Family play technique;

Identity Disorder and, 145; nightmares in response to, 75, 76; during toilet training, 87, 89, 91, 92, 100
Structure: for hyperactivity, 24; for Pervasive Developmental Disorders, 51
Substance use/abuse: adolescent, 10; maternal, 1; parental, 1
Sudden infant death syndrome (SIDS), 79
Support groups. *See* Parent support groups
Symbiosis, 15, 16
Symbolic identification, 174
Symbolization, in play therapy, 168, 173–174. *See also* Play therapy; Play therapy for abused children

T
Teacher education, about temperament, 6, 8
Temper tantrums: in autism, 28, 39; and impulse control, 20; in rapprochement stage of separation-individuation, 17; in toilet training, 86. *See also* Control; Defiance
Temperament, 2–10; and attachment, 16, 17; and Attention-Deficit/Hyperactivity Disorder, 9–10; classifications of, 4–5; defined, 3; dimensions of, 3; goodness of fit and, 5–7, 25; impulsivity and, 21, 22; in preschool-age children, 7–8; role of, 2; school functioning and, 8–9; significance of, 10, 25; sleep problems and, 61–62, 63, 68. *See also* Difficult temperament; Distractibility; Easy temperament; Impulsivity; Slow-to-warm-up temperament
Termination: of family play therapy, 180, 181; of play therapy for abused children, 175
Terrible twos, 20–21. *See also* Defiance; Impulse control; Temper tantrums

Therapeutic relationship: with family of abused children, 175, 181; with family of child with feeding disorders, 204; in play therapy with abused children, 170–172
Therapists: countertransference issues of, 108–109, 150, 182; immersion for, *xvii–xviii*; preparation of, *xvi–xviii*
Thienemann, M., 83
35 and Up, xvii
Thomas, A., 2–5, 10, 63
Threshold of response, as temperament trait, 3
Time givers, 71
Toddlers: adaptation of, to abuse, 164–165; development of, *xv–xvi*; impulse control and, 20–24; sleep requirements of, 65; sleep stages and patterns of, 63–67; toilet training of, 83–87; vulnerability of, to abuse, 159–161. *See also* Development; Preschool children
Tofranil, 54
Toilet training, 83–87; age of commencing, 84, 86; child-oriented approach to, 84–85; from child's perspective, 83–84; combined approach to, 86–87; do's and don'ts of, 86–87; encopresis and, 100, 103; enuresis and, 91, 93; methods of, 84–87; one-day behavioral method of, 85–86; parent-child battles over, *xvi*
Tonsillectomy, 78
Tourette's disease, 79
Transference issues, in feeding disorders treatment, 203–205
Transitional objects, *xvi*, 63; co-sleeping and, 74–75; cultural variables in, 74. *See also* Self-soothing aids
Translocation, 49
Transsexualism, 143, 157
Trauma: and co-sleeping incidence, 74; encopresis caused by, 100; in feeding disorder etiology, 191; of